MEETING
OUR MULTIFAITH
NEIGHBORS

MEETING OUR MULTIFAITH NEIGHBORS

Brice H. Balmer

Afterword by Stanley W. Green

Herald Press
Waterloo, Ontario
Scottdale, Pennsylvania

Library and Archives Canada Cataloging in Publication
Balmer, Brice H., 1944-
 Meeting our multifaith neighbors / Brice H. Balmer.

Includes bibliographical references.
ISBN 0-8361-9339-3

 1. Christianity and other religions. 2. Religious pluralism—
Christianity. I. Title.

BR127.B295 2006 261.2 C2006-902151-1

Photos in this book were taken by Mirko Petricevic, religion reporter and photographer for *The Record*, a daily newspaper in Kitchener-Waterloo, Ontario. He has worked with Interfaith Grand River to increase public awareness of faith communities in the region through his articles and photography.

Unless otherwise indicated, the Bible text is from the *New Revised Standard Version Bible*, Copyright ©1989, by the Division of Christian Education of the National Council of the Churches of Christ in the USA, and is used by permission.

MEETING OUR MULTIFAITH NEIGHBORS
Copyright © 2006 by Herald Press, Scottdale, Pa. 15683
    Published simultaneously in Canada by Herald Press,
    Waterloo, Ont. N2L 6H7. All rights reserved
Library of Congress Catalog Card Number: 2006011536
Canadiana Entry Number: C2006-902151-1
International Standard Book Number: 0-8361-9339-3
Printed in the United States of America
Book design by Sandra Johnson
Cover by Sans Serif
Cover photo by Mirko Petricevic © 2002 *The Record*, Waterloo Region, Ontario,
Canada
All other photos by Mirko Petricevic © 2001-2005 *The Record*, Waterloo Region,
Ontario, Canada

12 11 10 09 08 07 06   10 9 8 7 6 5 4 3 2 1

To order or request information, please call
1-800-759-4447 (individuals); 1-800-245-7894 (trade).
Web site: www.heraldpress.com

*To my friends who are part of Interfaith Grand River
and to the many people of different faiths
in the Waterloo, Ontario, region.*

CONTENTS

INTRODUCTION

Faith is a lived reality, and individuals often become curious as well as introspective when meeting neighbors of different religions. We study faith and religions through theology, world religions, the Bible, spirituality, and history. But do we know what skills, attitudes, and disciplines are appropriate for meeting our new neighbors?

Today in North America, many are facing a new situation. People of many religions live in one neighborhood, often in cities. How do we as Christians interact with and engage neighbors of other faiths? We expect to have interfaith experiences when traveling the world, but now the world has come to North America and will be here permanently. The Muslim or Hindu down the street from us has purchased the house where he lives and may be here longer than we are.

Many of us, especially those from rural areas and small towns in North America, grew up in a Christian environment with little exposure to other religions. The religious differences among our neighbors remained within the spectrum of Christianity: Catholic, Protestant, Pentecostal, Orthodox, or perhaps Seventh-day Adventist. We may have met Jehovah's Witnesses and Mormons in our communities too. We thought ourselves heterogeneous and thought we knew much about differences.

Now we find differences to which we are becoming accustomed: culture, race, religion, gender, economic class, and so on. Our neighborhoods are more colorful and diverse. Gradually we learn to talk with our neighbors, becoming friends in some instances. Our children and the children in our churches have learned to mix with the people around them at school, on athletic teams, and in the playground. They accept diversity as part of their environment.

But we adults often find that prejudices and negative stereotypes emerge in our thinking. We hope that these attitudes do not show in our speech and body language. We feel guilty because we want to be accepting and tolerant, but it does not come automatically. And we want to work through our questions, prejudices, and concerns in order to meet our neighbors and befriend them.

We face a new day. The migration of refugees, students, businesspeople, and workers of all sorts has altered North American demographics since the 1960s, when immigration restrictions were eased in both Canada and the United States. Before that, both countries made immigration difficult and prevented some peoples from entering.

- Asians were often severely restricted. Chinese men were allowed to come to build railroads, but could not become citizens. Regulations made it difficult or impossible for them to bring their families to North America.
- Few people from India and Pakistan could immigrate, even as citizens of the British Commonwealth. Africans found it difficult to remain, even after obtaining an education in Canada or the United States.
- Some Japanese families had immigrated to the West Coast but were interred during World War II. Many lost their homes, businesses, and truck farms without compensation.
- A boatload of Jews was turned away from Canada just before World War II. Even though Jewish citizens knew of

Hitler's activities and asked the government to allow the refugees to settle, the refugees were not admitted.

Though there was always some immigration, legal immigrants were primarily Caucasian and European, and mostly Christian. And some people of color and with different religions were allowed into Canada by virtue of being subjects of the British Commonwealth.

Today governments have a stronger sense of responsibility toward refugees, sponsoring some and allowing religious congregations to sponsor others. There is often compassion toward those who've fled persecution, oppression, or war in their homeland. Refugees have come from South America, Southeast Asia, Central America, the Middle East, and Africa.

Globalization has not only been about investment and business, but also about the movement of peoples throughout the world. Immigration to North America has increased in the last fifty years. People have fled unsafe situations, particularly refugees. Others have sought economic opportunities.

Many students are admitted into our universities and colleges and then settle here permanently. Some return to their homeland and then apply to emigrate to North America with their marketable skills. Western nations are realizing that they need immigration to keep their populations stable. Low birth rates in Europe and North America mean declining populations.

Churches, which often sponsor refugees, can be welcoming and hospitable. Sometimes entire congregations provide sponsorship, but often just a few actually have direct contact with the refugees, because some members may choose not to be involved. Though residents of a neighborhood do not choose when an immigrant family moves in, many feel the need to be friendly and welcoming. As long-term residents of the city, we Christians become hosts to strangers from different cultures, practicing other religions, and we need to be hospitable.

Because we may be unfamiliar with the visitors' culture or religion, we often feel uncomfortable and do not know how we will be accepted or what might offend. Yet we Christians are to strive to be good hosts to our newer neighbors.

Neighbors often learn about each other's foods, customs, country of origin, traditions, and language when they start talking about everyday activities, such as shopping and what schools their children attend. Since faith is important to Christians, we wonder about our new neighbors' religions. Can we ask about this? Can we talk about our own faith? Would it be acceptable to attend their religious services? Many questions emerge, but we encounter our culture's barriers to talking about religion. How do we find out what the new neighbors think or what they want to talk about?

Meeting Our Multifaith Neighbors has been written to help Christians openly discuss their faith in a way that respects another person's religion. As the conversation continues, a spiritually mature person of another religion becomes a trusted friend.

LISTENING TO OTHERS: DISCERNING THE TRUTH

Today there are many interpreters of other religions, and many books on religion have appeared since September 11, 2001, especially about Islam. We want to be informed but must also be aware of the writer's perspective. Media images can feed into racial and religious tensions within our nations and make us more fearful. But the media can also help us understand these complex situations. We need help to discriminate among the messages we hear.

Many Christians have little personal contact with Muslims, Jews, Buddhists, Sikhs, Hindus, or practitioners of other religions. This can make it difficult to counteract or diffuse media portrayals of these faiths. Christians might feel uncomfortable talking with a Hindu or Sikh to obtain a personal viewpoint on crises in India or to ask a Muslim about events in Iraq or

Afghanistan. How do Christians find out more about the communities their new neighbors have come from?

A 2001 census in Illinois[1] showed that there are about 350,000 Muslims and the same number of Methodists in the state. While most Christians in Illinois probably know many Methodists and are familiar with some issues in the Methodist church, how many know enough Muslims to develop a perspective on issues in the Islamic faith? Yet an informed Christian needs to know both Muslims and Methodists to understand the environment in Illinois. The struggle is to find contacts and information sources to expand awareness as well as friendships.

All individuals and groups have perspectives and biases, even when they try hard to be objective. Can Christians be clear about their experiences and honest about their lack of knowledge? If Christians are able to be vulnerable, they can also ask others to share their perspectives. Christians do not have to agree with their neighbors, but should always respect them. Each person in the conversation needs to sort out what is fact and what is opinion as friendships develop and they learn to work together with respect. How do we decide who we listen to? How do we begin to understand "the other"?

It is easy for individuals to be offended when someone who is not part of the religious community does the reporting. An outsider's interpretation of our community or of specific events can miss nuances and important background. Sometimes a reporter or writer comes with a particular perspective that is apparent in his or her writing, but bias may not always be so apparent. Cynthia Mahmood, an anthropology professor from Notre Dame University and the Kroc Institute, and an expert on terrorism and fundamentalist groups in South Asia, spoke at a 2002 St. Jerome's University forum in Waterloo, Ontario. There she reported that she had traveled in the mountains of Afghanistan and Pakistan and met members of the Taliban and other radical groups. Though some circumstances were dangerous, she was respected because she treats those she met with dignity.

At the forum, Mahmood questioned the perspectives and opinions of those commentators who have never been in Afghanistan or Pakistan, have never met a member of the Taliban or other radical groups, and have taken most of their information from other North American sources. How can these experts understand the complexities without encountering individuals involved in the struggles? In contrast to Mahmood and her extensive research and field experience, media organizations often do not allow staff to take time for understanding and dialogue with individuals and groups in the news. The news and commentary can then become significantly distorted, reporting only what appears on the surface.

As we consider getting to know our multifaith neighbors, it helps to remember that even Mennonites face frustrating and embarrassing situations when people don't take the time to get to know them. A Mennonite friend of mine recently sat, listening and silent, while a non-Mennonite talked at length about "the Mennonites," yet missed many nuances and was oblivious to the diversity within the Anabaptist community and its various denominations. My friend was perplexed and deeply offended. Should he contradict the speaker? Should he identify himself as a Mennonite and then become "the authority" and have the conversation focus on him?

Also, many Mennonite elementary-school students in Waterloo Region dread the day when a teacher explains Mennonites but talks primarily about Old Order Mennonites and Amish. Do these students identify themselves as Mennonite and explain that they do not wear plain dress or come to school in a horse and buggy or live in homes without electricity? Most remain unidentified in class. Some later talk with their parents or Sunday school teachers, but they often do not know how to handle this situation publicly or within themselves.

Sikhs, Buddhists, Muslims, Jews, Hindus, Unitarians,

Quakers, and others look forward to conversations and occasions when they can explain their beliefs in a safe environment in which others listen and ask questions in order to understand. Some have taken world religion classes in high school or college. That is good background, but people of faith often want to talk about worship, spirituality, prayer, beliefs, congregational life, and personal encounters with God. In a safe place, with people who can be trusted, they are delighted to explain the essence of their faith. They enjoy answering questions and breaking stereotypes, and many are anxious to make friends across religious boundaries. They have often been frustrated when the media perpetuate stereotypes, give quick explanations, or reinforce prejudices. They are delighted to be in a place where all are respected.

We must prepare ourselves to listen, to walk alongside, and to tell our own faith stories and answer the questions of others. As we engage our neighbor, we begin a new journey of understanding and affirming our own faith.

WHAT IS THIS BOOK?

Meeting Our Multifaith Neighbors is a spiritual journey written from the perspective of spirituality and pastoral theology. I'm hopeful that readers will develop new insights, overcome fears, and feel more comfortable expressing their beliefs and values in respectful conversations with neighbors of other faiths.

Biblical studies, systematic theology, and history are all important in multifaith dialogue and serve as background for interfaith discussion, though we need not be aware of all the arguments and doctrines in order to have a conversation about faith with our neighbor. To foster trust and friendship, we need to listen and present honest questions in a respectful way. Conversations with the neighbor may provide an impetus to study religion and theology in order to answer each other's questions.

This is not a book of world religions. There are many

resources we can use to learn about the history, theology, and practices of other religions, including books[2] and websites of faith communities. We need to be sure the website has been built and designed by an organization from that religion, not by another faith community. Currently there are hundreds of websites on Islam. You may need to consult a Muslim neighbor in order to navigate them. Two kinds of sites are listed in this book: those developed by individual faith communities and those developed by multifaith organizations. Because many religions have smaller populations in North America or have of diversity within their traditions, there may not be a website.

This is also not a book about multiculturalism, though religion is an important aspect of a culture. The skills, attitudes, and ideas in this book are meant to help the reader with cross-cultural encounters, because respect and mutual listening are critical for these meetings. In North America, many cultures reside, and specific organizations are working at multicultural activities and exchanges.

Many cultures and traditions are found within each major religion. At prayer in the Waterloo Sunni mosque, one finds men and women from twenty to thirty countries with much diversity of language. But they all pray shoulder-to-shoulder in Arabic. Waterloo Region, the area of southern Ontario consisting of Waterloo, Kitchener, and Cambridge, also contains mosques from other Muslim denominations, such as Shi'a and Ismaili. Within all these groups are additional schools and traditions. The religion is Islam and all Muslims follow the Qur'an, which is read and recited in Arabic in all services. The diversity is significant but secondary.

When Interfaith Grand River (IGR) was founded in Waterloo Region, we stated that *faith* was key to our discussion and action. I would make a similar statement about this book: it is about multi*faith* neighbors, not multi*culturalism*. We often find it acceptable to talk about culture with others.

We discuss foods, customs, dress, home country, and so on. However, North American culture teaches us that it is unacceptable to talk about religion. Yet it is often a very significant aspect of our lives and the lives of our neighbors, and the basis on which many decisions are made. How can we not talk about something so important?

In pastoral theology, the tasks are to listen and to walk alongside believers, helping them to answer questions, find comfort, understand suffering, and heal where possible. This book takes seriously the journey each reader needs to make as the multifaith neighbor is engaged, whether that neighbor is a co-worker, family member, friend, teacher, boss, or fellow student.

The reader will see where I locate myself in the midst of multifaith action and discussion. I have a perspective based on experience, as well as reflection and reading. My goal is to open doors to help the reader imagine, feel, pray, and think in safety and freedom. This opening can lead to spiritual transformation and an affirmation of values, ideals, and beliefs.

I can't know the experiences of readers, but I do know that movement into the multifaith world begins with questions, a little fear, a need to overcome prejudices and stereotypes, and a sense of being in new territory. I hope that you have a personal resolve to move into discussions with others who can walk with you on this journey to better understanding and friendship. We need Christian accompaniment as we face new experiences. The interfaith journey can be transforming and life-giving, since transformation is in essence spiritual. Christian friends can help us along.

When we encounter a person of another faith who is deeply spiritual, we often face many new questions. We see some reality in a new way. As we feel safe, we begin to wonder. As we work through various questions, we suddenly find ourselves transformed.

Transformation deepens our faith instead of watering it down.

If we engage in an ongoing conversation, neighbors may ask about our faith and we will want to answer their questions. The conversations move forward in a positive way for both people.

But if our prejudices and stereotypes dominate, or if we become afraid and rigid, we walk away from what could have been a rich and profound spiritual experience for our neighbor and for ourselves. We may need to walk away for a time because the situation and circumstances are so new and different that we are confused and frightened. But we can return and continue the journey later.

MY OWN EXPERIENCE

Growing up during the fifties and sixties in Bluffton, Ohio, I did not meet many people from other religions. Bluffton College had students from other countries, but most were Christian, and they were usually from places where Mennonites had workers. There was a small Roman Catholic church, which provided perhaps the greatest contrast to my own environment during that era. But it was a contrast only on Sunday morning because we all went to the public schools. The only time we students noticed this difference was when some of the Catholics were not allowed to attend the religious education classes sponsored by the Protestant churches in the community.

After college, I began working in large urban areas, where I met Jews who were neighbors or fellow teachers or members of peace and civil rights organizations to which I belonged. When I was in voluntary service with Mennonite Central Committee, I worked with Metropolitan Area Religious Coalition of Cincinnati, which included Catholics, Jews, Protestants, Quakers, and Unitarians. In the 1960s in Cincinnati, Islam and the Asian religions did not yet have significant populations, places of worship, or faith leaders who participated in multifaith discussions and action.

I often sat in on conversations in which religious leaders

debated topics of concern to the city. I also had the opportunity to attend at the Reform synagogue, including a Friday evening service. The prayers, the singing, and the sermon added a new dimension to my experience, even beyond what I later learned about Judaism in a seminary classroom. When I visited Jewish families in their homes, we often talked about our faiths around the table.

In seminary, I took a course on Judaism, taught by a rabbi who increased my understanding and appreciation of the Old Testament. A history course on the Orthodox and Eastern Christian faith communities helped me see the breadth of Christianity. More recently I've had opportunities to attend worship and to talk with these Christians about their faith and religious practices, which brought Orthodox Christian spirituality alive for me.

After 1975, refugees from Southeast Asia began moving into the Westside neighborhood of Denver, where I was a community minister. Though some Vietnamese were Catholic, many Vietnamese and Laotians were Buddhist, while the Hmong were primarily animist. Through Head Start and other community programs, we began to adapt support services culturally to meet the needs of the new residents, which often included their religious needs. But because many had limited English skills, it was difficult to interact.

During this time, our Mennonite congregation sponsored a Vietnamese mother with five children. She was Buddhist, and the family came to church irregularly. I began to probe the differences in our faiths, but she was more interested in learning how to assimilate and to know her sponsors better. Respect included letting her set the agenda.

I arrived with my family in Kitchener in 1979. In the late 1970s, Canada had begun accepting Southeast Asian refugees. In 1981, the Hmong accepted an invitation to move their Hmong Christian congregation into the church building where

I was a congregational pastor. English services were in the morning, Hmong services in the afternoon. The Hmong church leaders wanted to know more about being Mennonite. As they told me about their culture and religion and how they struggled against old animist beliefs since becoming Christian, many biblical passages and stories came more alive for me. Some of the Hmong marriage and family customs paralleled ancient Hebrew practices. As they experienced God's love and the break from fear, I heard questions similar to those of early Christian that Paul addressed in his letters. We worked together and learned from each other.

In the late 1980s and throughout the 1990s, Canada became the destination for refugee and immigrant groups from Central America, the Middle East, Africa, Asia, and the former Yugoslavia. Other immigrants came from China, India, the Caribbean, and Europe to establish businesses or to attend universities. At the ceremony where I became a Canadian citizen in 1986 were forty others from twenty-six countries.

As religious communities grew, immigrants purchased or built Sikh Gurdwaras, Buddhist and Hindu temples, Muslim mosques, and Jewish synagogues. Waterloo Region was transformed into a much different landscape.

House of Friendship, where I've worked since 1984, is a large agency serving economically and socially marginalized people. Throughout the 1990s, we saw more and more requests for vegetarian and halal (food permissible under Islamic law) emergency food hampers. As chaplaincy director, I have often sought the help of imams from local Sunni and Shi'a mosques to assist Muslims with programs such as English classes and parent-support programs. The imams and other Muslim volunteers have provided in-service training for our staff and donated the halal food we've needed for the hampers.

House of Friendship staff was concerned about which Muslim practices were cultural and which were central to

Islam. Two imams came to help discern how to approach some of the family problems our Muslim participants were facing. After September 11, some Muslim parents did not allow their children to play outdoors. An imam came to one of the community centers, so Muslims would feel safe there and non-Muslims could ask questions about Islam.

In the spring and summer of 2001, the Kitchener Waterloo Council of Churches contacted other faith groups to begin what came to be called the Interfaith Grand River. It was a brave new step for the council. IGR was organized so that faith leaders knew each other and could act together in a community crisis. The group spends the first hour of each meeting discussing a topic, such as the essentials of worship, how to pray, the role of the spiritual leader, justice, forgiveness, the functions of older people in the congregation, singing and chanting, practices at time of death and dying, and so on. The second hour is spent discussing community issues, organizational issues, or specific events that IGR coordinates.

The discussion hour at IGR has been wonderfully intense and refreshing. We learn about each other and discover both the convergences and divergences of our faith traditions. Each participant has grown as we listen to the others and then interpret our own tradition's perspectives on a particular topic. Many who have visited are intrigued and inspired by the discussions, and there is always much to ponder after the meeting.

In the IGR business hour, we have planned peace walks and multifaith prayer services, met with leaders from other sectors (schools, police, hospitals, social services), discussed violence to graveyards during an Easter weekend, talked with representatives of the media. We have also helped place rooms for meditation and study at a local hospital and two local universities.

The friendships in IGR have been stimulating, as have the visits to temples, mosques, Gurdwaras, synagogues, meditation centers, and churches. Through these, I have been transformed.

I am more profoundly Christian and Mennonite, even while studying, reflecting, and praying differently. The deep spirituality and connection with God that I observe around the IGR circle have allowed me to see that God has been working among many peoples through the centuries. I have become more accepting and can listen as others talk about their spirituality and their faith communities. Often I find I am reading the Bible, theology, and history with eyes more open to other perspectives within the Bible. I see how other IGR participants might see a particular passage or topic.

The summer before I wrote this book, Renison College professor Darrol Bryant and I taught a theology class at Conrad Grebel University College called "Encountering Our Multifaith Neighbors," in which students learned about other religions by experiencing worship and participating in discussions with religious leaders. Through pondering their own beliefs and faiths, the students were being transformed and growing spiritually. Each afternoon they were tired and yet enthusiastic about the next day's venture. A number of students had taken a world-religions course, but as we went to places of worship and met participants and leaders, their sense of the spirituality and faith of these multifaith neighbors grew. Many times while worshipping with other faiths, students were moved spiritually, though moments of polite disagreement occurred in conversations with religious leaders. The students learned to appreciate and communicate respectfully with members of other faiths.

I am hopeful that this book will assist the reader in engaging his or her multifaith neighbor in a similarly respectful way, so both the reader and the neighbor can grow spiritually.

QUESTIONS FOR DISCUSSION

1. What is your greatest concern as you meet neighbors of other faiths?

2. What are your hopes as your neighborhood or city becomes more religiously diverse?

3. Why did you decide to read this book? Do you have specific personal goals as you read and discuss this material?

4. What faith communities have settled in your city? When did they first arrive? What were the specific reasons these immigrants left their homeland? Are their faith communities growing by additional immigration? (Perhaps you can obtain statistics about your city or region. A census does not always gather religious data, but a social planning council or local university may have collected this information.)

5. Have you, your friends, or fellow church members met any recent immigrants? What religious traditions do they represent? Can you talk about your experiences of these meetings? What have you learned about yourself or about others through these experiences?

6. Where might individuals meet people of other faiths in your neighborhood? Schools, shopping centers, recreation programs, family and friendship networks, community activities?

7. Are there classes, seminars, and other opportunities in the city to learn more about other religions?

—1—
SPIRITUALITY AND TRANSFORMATION

Spirituality is an all-embracing concept. Carolyn Gratton says spirituality for humans is like water for fish.[3] How do we define something so intrinsic to our lives? The Hebrew people saw God's Spirit as breath or wind—difficult to observe even though we feel and see its results around and within us. Spirituality is about lived faith, so it is the core of all faith traditions. We perceive a person's spirituality from his or her attitudes, practices, and relationships: Is he or she relatively content? Has the person struggled to find balance and understanding through life's predicaments and questions? As I sit at interfaith discussions, I am often impressed by the spiritual maturity and profound questions or statements of other participants. I sense that they have breathed deeply of God's Spirit and contemplated our human predicament in profound and personal ways.

In discussions with church members, those recovering from addictions, and those working in healthcare, I use several definitions for spirituality and have pinpointed some of its characteristics, as found in a variety of interfaith experiences.

Spirituality is about love. It is difficult to measure spiritual growth and maturity, especially if one has struggled with religion or been abused and shamed. *Love* is a concept that all religions practice with different words and understandings. These four questions can help people look at their spirituality and growth:

1. Do you love yourself? Self-love is not narcissism. Jesus said, "Love your neighbor as yourself." We need to love ourselves in order to be open to our neighbor.
2. Can you freely give and receive love from another individual without manipulation?
3. Is there a place for you in this created world? Can you walk in the park and enjoy the world around you? Can you hear birds sing? Do you wonder as nature changes with the seasons?
4. Do you love a power greater than yourself and do you feel love within yourself from that higher power? Does your relationship with God provide support as well as guidance? Do you pray, and is prayer meaningful to you?

As we draw closer to God, we become more loving of self, others, the world, and God. Some spiritual directors use the word *spacious*, while therapists talk about *openness* when they speak of having room within ourselves to be generous and understanding, to be respectful, to entertain new ideas, and to listen carefully to others, to the world, and to God.

I asked the questions above using Alcoholics Anonymous (AA) language because I believe it is concrete and specific enough for Christians and others to use to gauge their own spirituality and growth. Members of twelve-step groups would counsel acceptance and tolerance in place of continuing attempts at trying to control events and people.

Concepts of love of self, others, the world, and a power greater than ourselves are at the heart of most faiths. AA comes primarily out of the Christian expression, but as I use this definition of spirituality I find people of other faiths use different terms while working with very similar questions.

For instance, IGR spent several meetings discussing The

Earth Charter of the United Nations,[4] which connects ecology, creation, and the dignity of people and all creation with spiritual practices. The concept has its origins in Buddhist traditions, but is easily affirmed by most religions. Though it speaks primarily to love of the world and our place in it, concern for self, other humans, and a power greater than ourselves is implicit in the charter.

Spirituality is a journey. Psychologist Erik Erikson and others tell us there are stages of human development. James Fowler and others define stages of growth in spiritual maturity.[5] Both point to progressive steps for individuals who are able to grow emotionally and spiritually through the phases. Because of personal trauma or abuse, individuals become "stuck" with particular tasks on the journey. They may be unable to take the risks necessary to grow. Congregations can be safe places where individuals can grow in faith, even as the congregation itself is "on a journey." Most congregations are intergenerational, so wisdom from various perspectives is shared. On the other hand, the congregation is a group of people growing and changing as the corporate faith engages the ethos of the larger community, social trends, and the personal achievements and crises of its members. The congregation is particularly important for many faith groups who have moved to North America and are adjusting as a group to a different social ethos.

The spiritual journey is not an easy road. Religious wisdom from many faith traditions tells us that suffering is an important teacher. Formerly conceived answers no longer resonate or bring comfort as we suffer or confront change. Family, friends, a supportive congregation, a small group, or spiritual practices may help us to resolve the angst and move to the next stage of our faith journey. We experience transformation.

A fifty-year-old friend of mine recently went through a grief process because he was dying. We talked about his concerns and fears, especially about missing family and friends. A month or so before he died, he said to me, "I'm not afraid of death. I will be with my father and brother. I just do not want to miss all the future events with my wife and children."

He has died peacefully, and not in isolation. Friends, family, co-workers, and church members supported him and each other. A whole community of people was on this spiritual journey together. At his funeral, the church was full as we sought to support one another and understand God's presence, or seeming absence, during that difficult time. My friend's family have felt community in many ways since his death.

People who are new to North America often do not realize how much their faith journey will be disrupted. Animists from Southeast Asia struggle when the first members of their community die a long way from their ancestors, because they believe that, in order for the spirits of the deceased to connect with the ancestors, the body needs to be buried relatively close to the ancestors' graves. Some want bodies to be buried on the southwest side of a hill, so the sun shines on the soul of the deceased and it more easily finds its way back to Southeast Asia. Graveyards in North America are not designed for this request. Some ask, "Can the spirits of the deceased cross the oceans?" Other beliefs hold that the body needs to be buried close to where the person is born and where their placenta is buried. The whole community struggles to understand this new environment and how the souls will reconnect. Flying a body back to the homeland may be too expensive or the deceased or the living may not be welcome there.

But transformation can happen when people witness a way of life better than the one in which they operate. Individuals often join churches because they like what they observe in worship or in community service. A number of new members reported to me that they joined the congregation where I was pastor because of the activities during the week and services in Spanish and Hmong. "If this church accepts all these people during the week and for services," they say, "there is a place for me. I want to be part of this congregation." A number of Hmong people join First Hmong Mennonite Church because Jesus Christ breaks the power of the "spirits" that produce fear.

At each stage, an important question to reflect on privately and with others is, "What do these experiences teach me about myself, other people, the world, and God?" The believer comes to Scriptures, religious practices, and the community for wisdom, discernment, and faith. The tasks of helping others grow spiritually often falls on those who are older because they have been through that particular portion of the journey already.

Though one can receive counsel from others and needs a supportive community, an individual walks the journey with God alone. At a recent interfaith meeting, a Muslim woman asked for advice and prayers because she was being harassed by tenants in her apartment complex. She could no longer sit on her small patio. Several Christians offered to advocate for her, contact the police, and make this a human-rights concern. The Buddhist monk in the group said quietly, "As a Buddhist, I would ask you what this suffering means and what you can learn from it." Another group participant said that she should move to another apartment.

What should the Muslim woman do? How does her Muslim community support her? How does she grow spiritually on this phase of her journey? The advice of the interfaith community is important and demonstrates the ways each community deals with suffering, but she must find the solution within her own faith and her religion.

Spirituality is living out our values, ideals, and beliefs. People develop and articulate values, ideals, and beliefs as a result of their interactions with others, their experiences, their education, and their observations. It is spiritually essential that they live them out.

People in a new environment, specifically someone new to North America, will struggle to live out their values, ideals, and beliefs. There will be new circumstances and predicaments in which they will need to be careful or even question what to do. For example, a Muslim who has lived in a country where Muslims are in the majority does not worry about whether meat is halal.[6] Most butcher shops and restaurants back home would have only halal product. In a restaurant or grocery store in North America, a Muslim likely won't find halal meat and may worry that other products contain pork derivatives.

In addiction recovery, we use the term *negative spirituality*, which means that a person's lifestyle and actions are contradictory to his or her values, ideals, and beliefs. *Positive spirituality* is living out one's beliefs, values, and ideals, but some who are abused face a profound struggle in finding a spiritual and ethical core. When people are shamed because of abuse and do not love themselves, they find it difficult to reflect on their life. Shamed people are often angry, resentful, and frustrated. Their behaviors are reactive, not chosen. When sober and in recovery, they need to remember and reflect on what they believe, what things and actions they valued, and what their ideals are. The spiritual journey to recovery is to act and live according to the messages deep within the self.

Refugees and immigrants struggle with negative spirituality in a different way. In the homeland, the whole community often observed religious practices. A person fit into the community and did not face ethical dilemmas about daily living.

For instance, Sikh men moving to North America often cut their hair and shaved. This means they are no longer accepted as Khalsa,[7] because they do not wear the five symbols of the Sikh tradition: uncut hair, turban, bracelet, special underwear, and kirpan (a knife). Their values and ideals would be to practice Khalsa and their faith, but they worry they will not be employed or will not be acceptable to their neighbors. At a

Sikh Gurdwara, there are many men with turbans, while many others have cut hair. All may come to worship and pray; all are part of the Sikh organization. But some are excluded from Khalsa. Their experiences and the North American ethos force them into a negative spirituality; they cannot practice what they believe and value.

People of all faiths have values, ideals, and beliefs. This is a good place to begin conversations with others. Religious training and family culture are often the source of these values. As two individuals from different traditions talk about their ideals or beliefs, they learn to trust each other and understand both faiths. Religion teaches us many core beliefs; the individual spiritual journey will confirm or test them. As we mature, these beliefs and values will change. After learning to trust the other person, we together will find deep resonance as we discuss our faith journeys, each guided by the beliefs and values of our own tradition.

TRANSFORMATION THROUGH ACTION AND REFLECTION

Transformation occurs when we grow or diminish spiritually. Each person is an individual, created in God's image. Therefore we do not need to fear transformation, especially if we are attempting to grow into the heart of God. Transformation will help us understand ourselves, our world, our suffering, and the difficult questions we face. We need not fear it, because even in the midst of suffering and angst, gentleness and spaciousness are characteristics of spiritual growth.

Spiritual directors are individuals who listen deeply to a person while also listening for the Spirit of God in the conversation. They ask themselves, "Are there biblical passages to help this person with this phase of the journey? How might he or she pray differently? How might this concern be seen spiritually?" Spiritual direction is spacious and gentle, and insightful and supportive, even when challenging. A person being directed spiritually should ask some serious questions if the spiritual director, pastor, or leader is being overly directive and not listening to his or her voice or for the presence of God in the conversation. Spiritual growth happens best when the spiritual director walks alongside and helps us discern the movement of God within.

But even with spiritual direction and other community support, we have our own work to do for our growth. As a person who has worked in many different and sometimes difficult situations, I like to use a spiritual action/reflection wheel often identified with liberation theology. Knowing that encountering the multifaith neighbor will be a new experience with many questions raised, I suggest the spiritual reflection wheel as a way of digesting the experience and being prepared for the next step of the journey with the neighbor. The wheel can be explained as follows:

Experience

Worship with Congregation   Personal Reflection

Praying   Reflection with Others

Reading & Seeking Information

- **The experience** is the first place on the wheel. All other steps can come in any order. Say that you meet a neighbor who is wearing what appear to be Indian clothes. You say hello and genuinely welcome him and his family to the neighborhood. His dress or physical characteristics alert you to the fact that he may be Hindu, but he could be Muslim, Christian, Jain, Buddhist, or of another faith, because India has been multifaith for several thousand years.

- **Personal reflection** is thinking about this experience. Is the other person pleasant and friendly? Is he shy? Are you comfortable or uncomfortable with him? Why? Have you met people from India before? Why do I think he is from India? It is important to take time to think about the experience and why it is different. Perhaps the most important function is to know what questions you have.

- **Reflection with others** may produce information about the family as well as more information that has not been part of the conversation. Perhaps other friends have had Indian people move into their neighborhood or have co-workers from the Subcontinent. A friend, family member, or church member may have lived in India. Questions can be taken to others for sorting out as well as concrete answers. This step is not gossip but discerning with others. It may be taken with another individual or in a group.

- **Reading and seeking information:** This is the time to read about India, Hinduism, Islam, or even migrations from India to North America. Diana Eck's *A New Religious America: How a "Christian Country" Has Become the World's Most Religiously Diverse Nation* (HarperSanFrancisco, 2002) is an excellent book about the major world religions coming to the United States. The Internet is also a good source of information.

- **Praying** with the experience in mind and heart may help you consider how God sees. Are you open to God's presence with you as you meet your neighbor? Silence can be a good prayer. Stating your confusion can be prayer as you look for answers. You may ask for your eyes, ears, mind, and heart to be opened, so you can sense God's presence in the world and direction for your life.

- **Worship with a congregation or smaller group** could be a time to share and discuss with friends. This would be different from group reflection and would include a time of prayer. Through prayer, worship, Scripture reading, and sermons, we as Christians open ourselves to God's guidance and presence in the world and to our participation in the kingdom.

- **The experience occurs again, and you start the reflection process over.** You may be the initiator of the new experience or you may wait for the next encounter. Hopefully the previous steps will help you know when and how to initiate or face the next experience.

One cycle of this reflection process could take a week or a month while at other times you will take the important steps in an hour. For example, you might decide to take a basket of fruit to the neighbor, because you would do that for any other person moving onto your street. This might happen the same day, perhaps a half-hour after your first meeting, when you've only had time for your own reflection and maybe a phone call to a friend. But you may feel uncomfortable and need more time for reflection or to meet with friends and church members for prayer, reading, and worship, so the next experience would not occur for a week or two.

This spiritual reflection wheel takes your life's journey as the context for spiritual growth. Group support, study and reflection, prayer, and worship enhance the next experience as well as your own journey.

Transformation occurs as we consciously reflect on our lives and see changes in our lifestyle, attitudes, and values. With the spiritual reflection wheel, we are serious about our own transformation as we move into the heart of God.

Transformation usually does not occur when we are first confronted with an issue or an experience. Rosemary Houghton has written about "moments of decision" when we have the opportunity to make a change that we think is good for us. Sometimes we have the opportunity but still behave as we normally would, even though we prefer to change. This may happen a number of times. Even as we keep old behavior patterns, we are building up the will and determination necessary to make a serious change.[8]

At some point, when an opportunity or difficulty arises, we move forward differently and may change something in our lifestyle.

∾

After coming to Canada, a male Sikh who is now a participant in IGR, cut his hair. He was in business and felt the need to be accepted by his customers as well as the vendors from whom he purchased raw goods. He has attended IGR for over a year and has felt accepted as a Sikh. He has seen others living out their values and beliefs, even when it distinguishes them as a member of a religious group. At the Gurdwara, he prays and talks with his friends. Many Sikhs in the Waterloo Region participate actively in the Gurdwara but are not Khalsa.

At one monthly IGR meeting, he appeared with his turban and was growing a beard and moustache. He said he had wanted to maintain Khalsa when he moved to Canada, but after not finding work for several months, he cut his hair and kept it cut for many years. He remained a faithful Sikh, but had forsaken the Khalsa tradition, which required wearing a bracelet, special underwear, a comb, and small sword called kirpan, and not cutting his hair. IGR gave him the extra support he needed to maintain these five Khalsa practices. He was grateful for the examples of others and for the acceptance he felt from the group.

This man made a significant transformation. His spirituality matured through with many "moments of decision." He now wears the outward signs of a Sikh, and his spiritual and organizational leadership at the Gurdwara has grown over the past two years. He has since been licensed by his Gurdwara and the local province to perform marriages.

The Bible contains many transformations, sometimes called conversions. I prefer to use the word *transformation*, which implies a deepening of faith. Others say that any person of faith is constantly being converted by fellow believers and by God.

Imagine Peter's spiritual transformation when he meets the centurion Cornelius in Caesarea, as recorded in Acts 10. As a Jew, Peter followed his religious law and did not associate with Gentiles. When he went to the roof to pray before lunch while in Joppa, he was unaware that he was about to experience a new chapter in his faith journey and in the Christian story. There he fell into a trance and had a vision in which unclean animals were lowered to him from heaven. God said, "Get up, Peter; kill and eat." Peter protested; he could not eat those unclean foods. God challenged him, "What God has made clean, you must not call profane" (vv. 13, 15).

Peter was confronted with a spiritual change but at first was unwilling to be transformed, even when confronted three times by God. In his moment of decision he sought to remain faithful to Jewish religious codes but was determined to follow God's voice. To change would mean to go against the society in which he lived and being perceived as unfaithful to God, even though it was God who requiring the transformation. To change meant a radical break from tradition and probably a confrontation with the other apostles in Jerusalem.[9]

After his vision, Peter was confronted by Cornelius's servants summoning him to go the centurion's home. He followed the movement of the Holy Spirit and traveled with the men. He still had questions, but he also had time to process the Spirit's urging.

Cornelius was so devout and virtuous that when he greeted Peter, he worshipped the apostle as a divine presence. After Peter put a stop to that, he recounted his dream for all in the household. The dream explained why he would enter the home of a Gentile. Cornelius then described his vision, and Peter preached the gospel of Jesus Christ. Cornelius and his household experienced the Holy Spirit coming upon them. Peter had wisely brought along six Jewish Christian witnesses and asked them whether any would deny baptism of Cornelius and his household. The household was baptized.

Peter and Cornelius and his household were transformed by the movement of the Holy Spirit. Peter had changed long-established habits and customs. But the transformation was not finished. As part of a community of Jesus followers that discerned God's movement in the post-resurrection days, Peter had to go back to Jerusalem and explain to the other apostles what had happened. He and his witnesses were persuasive. They had seen and experienced the Holy Spirit again just as at Pentecost. The council in Jerusalem accepted this report with caution and accepted the Gentiles' baptisms.

Can we see the Holy Spirit moving among other faith communities? Can we sense God's presence in other people's lives? Are we prepared for our own transformation as we sense deep faith within people of different cultures, customs, and religions? This story from Acts is about the transformations of Peter and Cornelius. It records the moment when Gentiles were welcomed into the early church as the Holy Spirit worked among them.[10] Cornelius's conversion helped open the church for Paul and missionaries who moved out of the Jewish communities and into the whole Roman Empire.

According to the Hebrew Scriptures, the prophet Jonah was not open to transformation either. He could not follow God and undertake the conversion of the people of Nineveh. Instead he wanted to hang on to his resentments and hoped that God would destroy those people and their city.

Each of us regularly has opportunities for transformation. But we are not always ready or open to moving forward. An initial negative response to transformation is not a final answer. In this prophetic book, Jonah had several opportunities for transformation.

Transformation occurs on a regular basis as individuals and faith communities experience the movement of God in new ways, as they adapt to the culture changing around them, as they respond to suffering or life-changing conditions, and as new questions arise. Hopefully transformation occurs in the midst of a significant spiritual reflection process.

The process of transformation is often complex. At a residential care program for older people, a table of men ate their meals together. Three men were Protestants and one was Mormon. The Mormon easily talked about his faith. He had been an active member and still attended worship but could not participate in other activities of the "stake"[11] because of his age and disabilities. Another man at the table had actively participated in his church for ninety years. He still attended chapel services and his children took him to church every Sunday. But the table conversations troubled him.

As chaplain, I talked with him many times. He had not anticipated thinking more profoundly about his faith at his age. He was unprepared to respond to his Mormon friend and dinner companions. So he sought out me and several others to walk with him because he needed other spiritual companions. The multifaith table conversations were a transformative experience for him. He was being transformed, but was not as susceptible to Mormon conversion as he'd initially feared. He died a faithful Christian.

All Christians need to find ways to continuously be open to transformation through a vertical dimension of faith, that is, a more profound awareness of God, Jesus Christ, and the Holy Spirit in their lives. Transformation also includes a horizontal dimension, living as people who love others. Self-transcendence—enhancing both the vertical and horizontal relationships while moving beyond one's own needs and desires—is essential to meet life situations and move spiritually deeper into the heart of God.

QUESTIONS FOR DISCUSSION AND REFLECTION

1. All people with active faith have times of transformation when they change thoughts, beliefs, behaviors, and practices because of congregational life, personal experiences, or their own perception of God's Spirit moving within them. Can you identify one or more times when you have been transformed?

2. Imagine yourself in a country where Christianity is not the primary religion. Which of your practices and beliefs do you think might be challenged? How would you move forward in faith? Would you seek out a Christian congregation in your area to assist you? How would you identify ways in which God is already at work among the people you meet and the culture around you?

3. Both Cornelius and Peter were devout followers of God. In praying, they were led by the Holy Spirit into new ventures that challenged their beliefs. Peter especially needed to sort out which traditions and practices were ordained by God. He may have chosen to continue to practice eating only clean foods, but he was not rigid or judgmental with Gentiles as he entered their homes, ate with them, and preached among them. As you mature and have new experiences, do you wrestle with what is the will of God in this time and place? Do we have to condemn the past as we change our viewpoints?

4. Which of your values, beliefs, and ideals are made stronger or are brought into question as you meet and engage in discussion with your multifaith neighbors?

5. Have you taken note of the spirituality of another person, particularly a person from another faith? What signs of spirituality are noticeable? As you talk with and get to know your neighbor, what inner integrity and faith emerges?

6. Are there beliefs, values, and ideals that you have difficulty practicing because of our culture? How do you justify not keeping these values and practices? Could you understand and befriend a person from another faith who also has difficulty practicing his or her beliefs and values in North America?

—2—

HOSPITABLE
AND INCLUSIVE

Being hospitable is highly valued in Christianity, but hospitality is much more expansive than the common perception involving overnight guests or meals with friends, family, and acquaintances. Hospitality is also far more than organizing social events in the church or community.

In Scripture, we read of Martha's hospitality. She prepared the meal while her sister talked with Jesus. Biblical hospitality reaches out to the stranger, even the enemy, and creates a safe place where all can learn to know each other, rest, and eat together. Jesus and his disciples were dependent on hospitality as they went from town to town. In Luke 19, Jesus invited himself to eat with Zacchaeus, an outcast because he was a tax collector. In Jesus' parables, marginalized individuals like the good Samaritan practiced hospitality to a stranger who had been robbed, beaten, and left for dead (see Luke 10:29-37).

Christine Pohl defines hospitality as the welcoming of strangers and a response to their physical needs for food, shelter, protection, and so on. Hospitality is the recognition of our common humanity and involves both the host and the guest.[12] The stranger, and even an enemy, is created in the image of God, according to Jack Suderman. But a sense of risk and danger is present when we meet each other. With hospitality one is

welcomed into a sanctuary, a safe place "for strangers and enemies to learn from each other."[13] God is present in this safe
place, which will now have enough light to overcome the dark-
ness of enmity between the host and guest. God is actually
ahead of humanity in the desire to befriend all who are made
in God's image. In taking the risk to be hospitable to the
stranger or the enemy, we find the joy of God's love and peace
in our midst.

In Genesis 18, Abraham welcomed strangers and provided
food and safe lodging for them. They turned out to be the
angels who announced that Sarah would have a child through
whom the covenant would be carried into future generations.

The Israelites were sojourners who wander with their family and animals. They had been in Egypt and the desert, and
then entered and settled in Palestine. The Torah frequently
commanded them to welcome strangers, aliens, and sojourners. In Deuteronomy 24:14-22, for example, we find instructions to care for outsiders as we would orphans and widows.
We're told to

- pay wages quickly and fairly to all, especially the poor
and aliens,
- practice justice with all people, and
- leave grain in the field and grapes in the vineyard for
orphans, widows, and aliens.

Deuteronomy 26:1-15 emphasizes generosity and fairness
toward those on the economic and social margins. The
Israelites were to remember that they were delivered from slavery and must express their gratitude by assisting others less fortunate.

In the New Testament, Luke 24 tells the story of the two
disciples of Jesus who talked with a stranger on their way from
Jerusalem to Emmaus after the crucifixion and resurrection.

They invited the stranger for a meal and overnight lodging and recognized him as Jesus in the "breaking of the bread."

In the Middle Ages, people welcomed pilgrims into their villages and homes. They did not know who among the beggars might be monks, nuns, or priests. They did not know whether these strangers might be angels bringing good news. Many villagers and farmers had little food or money, and very small homes, but they welcomed strangers into their communities and provided food and shelter.

Eleanor Epp Stobbe cites Letty Russell's definition of hospitality as being about diversity, pluralism, compassion absent the need for conversion and evangelistic outreach to others.[14] It is not about unity, uniformity, and exclusion. Rather, the community celebrates in the midst of people's differences and finds God's grace and hope.

Neighbors of other faiths are often treated as strangers and sometimes as enemies, especially when the media attaches terrorist labels to certain faiths or cultures. Many North Americans live in cultures dominated by Judeo-Christian values and norms, so they have little experience in other countries or with other religions. But North American Christians practice "hospitality to strangers" when they welcome multifaith neighbors.

We all have a tendency to fear strangers and worry about risks. Jesus recognized that his disciples confronted stereotypes, religious questions, and other barriers as they welcomed the marginalized into their midst. Is this person "clean" religiously? What will other people say if a Jew speaks to a Samaritan or a Roman, especially a soldier? Do I become marginalized because my friend is a tax collector? Can we trust people we don't know?

Differences can create tension between the individual and the larger community, which may want to exclude the stranger and maintain the status quo. The exclusive neighborhood often focuses on its own needs and concerns. It seeks to protect itself from outsiders. But Christians have another mandate: to follow examples from Abraham through Jesus and into the early church and be hospitable and inclusive. Christians break through fear and experience the joy of hospitality when they are welcoming and inclusive.

In *Becoming Human*, Jean Vanier cites fear as the primary motivator for exclusion.[15] We are afraid

- that the stranger or guest will not welcome us. We may be insecure and feel the stranger will not accept, tolerate, or be friendly with us. We do not want to be rejected.
- that we may need to change as the result of this relationship but do not know how to change. We wonder if the person from another faith has a better truth. We question some of our own beliefs and practices.
- because we have heard many stories about strangers from other people; we do not know what to believe. Prejudice is often at the root of this fear, especially when we have not had concrete experiences with individuals in a group being stereotyped. Sensational stories that do not include perspectives from our multifaith neighbors can also create fear.
- that we may lose power or status in the community. It is not only whether the other person will accept me, but also whether friends, family, church members, or neighbors will accept the new person, especially if he or she is from a different religion.

Marcus Borg uses the term "closed hearts" to talk about rigidity, rationalizing, and blindness to others and new options.[16] At the deepest level, the individual either cannot or will not be open to new people and ideas. Some resist because of fear. Others are not ready to change because they enjoy being on a plateau. Often insecurity is at the core of a closed heart, which Borg describes as one that is insensitive to freedom, preferring the status quo, and lacking the gratitude and compassion to accept new people and new ideas.

It is not only North American Christians who may have a closed heart and are unable to extend hospitality. Miroslav Volf in *Exclusion and Embrace* is concerned that hospitality and inclusion "entails a judgment against evil in every situation."[17] A safe place needs to be created. Individuals may be apprehensive of interfaith discussion, but no one should be in emotional or physical danger. Some individuals may imagine dangers that are not real, so they are apprehensive or fear participation. Moderators, facilitators, and planners should know participants well enough to make sure a group feels safe. In the neighborhood, individuals can gradually learn to know their neighbors through discussions across the fence, meeting each other on the sidewalk and exchanging greetings, and talking with others who know the neighbors or their friends. Trust builds slowly. Neighbors or group participants need time to appreciate differences and learn how their lives and concerns are similar. In the neighborhood, adults may learn to know each other because their children all attend the same school. With refugee sponsorship, committees and pastors may provide the congregation with education about the culture, religion, and customs of the family or individual. Leaders hopefully will address concerns of members, realizing that not all will be interested in providing hospitality and meeting this individual or family. The congregation as a whole is hospitable and protects the dignity of the sponsored refugees and the members.

In *Addiction and Grace*, Gerald May explains that freedom proceeds from love of self, others, and God. If we are too attached to ideas and practices, we do not have the freedom to love others. A wholesome love of self must exist for us to freely create the safe space where a stranger can be welcomed without conditions attached to the friendship. The spiritual exercise is to detach[18] ourselves from prejudices, stereotypes, and fears in order to create the freedom necessary to love the other person as we love ourselves. Jesus' commandment to love God and others as we love ourselves is the basis of our freedom. Self-love allows us to risk and then to love the other, especially the stranger and enemy.[19]

The Bible often talks about hardened hearts, such as that of Pharaoh or Herod. In the Gospels, Pharisees and other leaders are often described as having hardened hearts because they cannot see God's presence in Jesus. They did not have freedom in God's love and were attached to the status quo. They believed that salvation could be attained by following the law, and they encouraged others to imitate their ways in order to be acceptable. They were blind to God's work in the world and closed to the diversity of Gentiles, Samaritans, Romans, lepers, fishermen, and tax collectors in their neighborhoods. Did they fear Jesus as a leader who invited diversity by welcoming the marginalized and aliens? Did they worry about how they might have to change? Were they concerned by the risks to their positions or to Judaism and Israel? For Pharaoh, the risk was losing workers and slaves. For the Herods,[20] the risk at Jesus' birth and at the time of the crucifixion was losing his status with the Jewish people and with the Roman authorities.

Because of fear, insecurity, attachment, the risk of change, and concern for power, some do not welcome strangers; they find it difficult to be hospitable. They may set up roadblocks to keep their lives under control. So the hospitable North American Christian who wishes to welcome multifaith neighbors must have a mature spirituality and be connected to a congregation that nurtures a spirit of hospitality.

Anxieties, sensitivities, and feelings need to be recognized so that they do not become barriers in our relationships with our neighbors. Consider the following points:

It is all right to be apprehensive when there are many things about the stranger we do not know. We can trust God to walk with us as we learn to know the neighbor.

It is all right to worry about our innocent mistakes and errors. We are just beginning this experience. Our neighbors may have the same worries, and we can learn from each other.

We may be enthusiastic about our experience with our new acquaintances, but friends and associates may not share our excitement or our interest in learning more. This is all right. They may never have the opportunities or occasion to meet strangers. Or they may need to prepare to meet the stranger in their own style. Can we give them the freedom to do that?

Prejudices and stereotypes will enter our minds. We can put them on hold and evaluate them after our first meetings are finished. We can then talk about them with friends or associates in a safe setting, where others are hospitable and want to create a safe place.

∾

A Muslim imam comes into the room for an interfaith meeting, and one of the female leaders extends her hand in greeting. He politely says, "Men are not allowed to shake hands with a woman because we do not touch a person of the opposite sex unless she is a family member: wife, mother, daughter, sister, or aunt." The imam has been gracious and accepting: he gladly enters into the discussion with the other Christians and Muslims about future events and acknowledges the woman as leader of the Christian organization. Later the Christian participants talk about this exchange, remembering the graciousness of the imam and recognizing an important lesson. The Muslims and Christians have continued to work together with deep appreciation, even though mistakes are made. It is part of the process.

During the discussion, Christians learn that the Muslim organization has delivered some medicines and other supplies to Iraq at the same time as the Christian organization. Both groups are concerned about Iraqi children and civilians. Both oppose the war, though the political and theological rationales differ. Muslims ask if they can volunteer with the Christian organization and assist in preparing materials to be shipped overseas.

Ten people from each organization later meet at the mosque for a meal and discussion. Men and women enter the mosque through the doors for their gender and are in separate but adjacent sections. Since it is prayer time, the Muslims pray while the Christians sit on the floor against the back wall of the men's and women's sections. The Muslims prepare the food so halal is observed. After the meal, the discussion becomes difficult because of the wall between the men and women, so the imam asks the women to join the men on the men's side. He states that this is an exemption for that evening only. The discussion is interesting and helpful. Though divergence is obvious, many converging views are recognized and helpful as plans are made to meet again. Men and women leave through their separate doors.

The suggestion to meet was from the Christians; the decision to meet at the mosque was an invitation from the Muslims. Christians were observers at prayer, but most were quiet and praying, even while observing. The discussion was moderated by a Christian and a Muslim. Everyone felt a spirit of kinship at the end of the evening.

We can overcome our fears, take appropriate risks, put aside issues of status and power, and welcome the stranger. Marcus Borg talks about "thin places" where hearts, instead of being hardened, are opened so that the Spirit of God enters. He says then we experience grace and can accept change; we are being transformed.[21] We know that God is with us. Therefore fear, risk, and status have less impact and power in our decision making. Gerald May would say that we have the freedom to love because we experience grace and the presence of God in our lives.[22]

THE BOOK OF RUTH

Naomi and her husband, Elimelech, were in Moab because of the famine in Israel. Their sons married Moabite wives. Unfortunately Elimelech and both sons died, leaving Naomi with two daughters-in-law. Because of her powerlessness and vulnerability in that foreign culture, she decided to return to Bethlehem by herself. One daughter-in-law, Ruth, decided to go to Bethlehem with her. She declared that she would stay with Naomi and worship the God of Israel all of her life. Yet in Bethlehem, Ruth was a foreigner and a person of another faith. How much prejudice and stereotyping in the community demeaned Ruth and limited her status is unknown. However, Naomi felt the need to protect her as much as possible. In Torah law, foreigners are to be treated with kindness, but there must have been dangers that Naomi saw.

Though Ruth was a foreigner, she was seen as industrious and caring. Her virtues were recognized by the workmen as she gleaned barley. The landowner, Boaz, was attracted to her and recognized his responsibility as a family member to Naomi and Ruth. Despite the Jewish tradition that Judaism descends from the mother, Ruth, a non-Jew, and Boaz were married. Ruth gave birth to a son who would be the grandfather of King David. God honored Boaz's hospitality toward the stranger, his keeping of family obligations toward a deceased cousin, and his willingness to risk having his children born to a Moabite woman.

The Interpreter's Bible summarizes the hospitality of God as portrayed in the book of Ruth as the "conviction of a God whose love overflows the limits good people seek to impose upon him, and who continually stretches the content of neighborhood and brotherhood until it embraces all lands and peoples."[23]

QUESTIONS FOR DISCUSSION AND REFLECTION

1. What are your first reactions to strangers in your neighborhood, especially if they are different from you culturally, racially, or religiously? Can you discuss these first reactions with a safe group, so they can be acknowledged? And can the group then help members understand where good and prejudicial reactions come from.

2. Recall an experience with an individual or family significantly different from you and yours. How did you open to this person or family as you shared experiences and learned to know them?

3. Can you describe times and people with whom you, your family, or your congregation practiced hospitality. What were your initial reservations, if any? What joy has emerged?

4. As you remember experiences of hospitality, what have you learned of God's love and graceful presence on those occasions?

A MULTIFAITH EXPERIENCE
Our Son Married a Muslim

The following is the synthesis of several interviews with a Mennonite couple in North America, whose son married a Muslim woman. First person is used because the couple has approved this telling of their experience.

Our son is a deeply committed Christian. At the Mennonite college he attended, he studied Bible and theology. He met his future wife, a committed Muslim, at college. She was also a Bible and theology major. She is very knowledgeable about the Bible and Qur'an. Both our son and daughter-in-law live highly moral lives and are very respectful of each other and their faiths.

Their engagement and marriage were not sudden. They dated at college, but when her parents saw that this was a serious relationship, they decided that she should come back home and perhaps go to a different college. The year apart did not decrease their love for each other. She came back to college and graduated.

It was four years from the time our son told us how serious the relationship was until they were married. After graduating from college, he worked another three years until they were married. After our daughter-in-law graduated, she worked one year before getting married. Since her family was prominent in their community, they had a formal engagement celebration, which her parents arranged. In her culture, the engagement was as important as the wedding. We were unable to attend. The wedding was at the college chapel and the two of them planned it carefully with the pastor. It was a very meaningful worship service.

We've gone through many stages as we've learned to accept this marriage. At first we were very emotional and worried about how a mixed marriage would work. We wanted the best for our son. We asked how he, who was baptized and took his Christian commitment so seriously, could marry a Muslim and remain Christian. We wondered about our grandchildren. What kind of faith would they have? We wondered if we could be ourselves as Christians with our grandchildren? We had many sleepless nights.

The second stage was learning to know other parents whose Christian children were married to Muslims. It was comforting to hear their stories, know about their struggles, and learn about their children's current lives. Several parents were prominent in the wider church. Our congregational and denominational family were very important to us, so we had wondered how others would accept us as well as our son and future daughter-in-law. We did not feel so alone or anxious after talking with other parents.

The third stage has been learning to know our future daughter-in-law, her religion and her culture. She is most delightful, and we have grown to love her. After their marriage, we visited the Middle East with them to experience a Muslim culture, one stricter than her own. We were in a number of Muslim homes there. While our daughter-in-law was careful to cover her hair with the hajib in public as well as keep essential Muslim practices, we started to realize how uncomfortable she was in a strict Muslim environment. She also had lived in North America for several years and was questioning some aspects of the Muslim culture, especially the status and lifestyle of many women. She was firm in her faith while also believing that women and men had dignity and the right to be active in vocations and in the political arena.

We met our future daughter-in-law's parents when she graduated from college, a year before the wedding. They had lived in the United States, so they understood the culture here. We learned we had several mutual acquaintances, which also helped us to relax.

As the wedding day approached, we visited some of our relatives to answer their questions. This went better than we'd expected. No one refused to attend the wedding, which was in the chapel at a Mennonite college. The processional was a traditional Muslim wedding march. Both the Bible and the Qur'an were used in the readings. It was a very worshipful event.

Covering the hair is an important aspect of Muslim modesty for women. Since we are her family, our daughter-in-law is more casual and relaxed with us and does not need to cover her hair. Yet she continues to be very careful to cover her hair when guests are at our home or when we go out.

We are very proud of both our son and daughter-in-law. They are individuals of integrity and are deeply committed to each other and to their faiths. We now see some of the constraints on her because of her family and their prominence in her culture. She respects her parents, her extended family, and her heritage.

We still have some questions and concerns, but we accept and love our daughter-in-law. We are thankful for the support of our friends and our church. We are sure that God loves our son and daughter-in-law, and we know they sincerely love and follow God.

QUESTIONS FOR DISCUSSION AND REFLECTION

1. Imagine yourself in the situation described above. What personal and theological issues would you need to address as a Christian?
2. What support would you need from your congregation? From friends and family?
3. If a friend or member of your congregation told you that his or her child was engaged to a person from another faith, how would you respond? What are your questions and issues? How can you reach out to your friend?

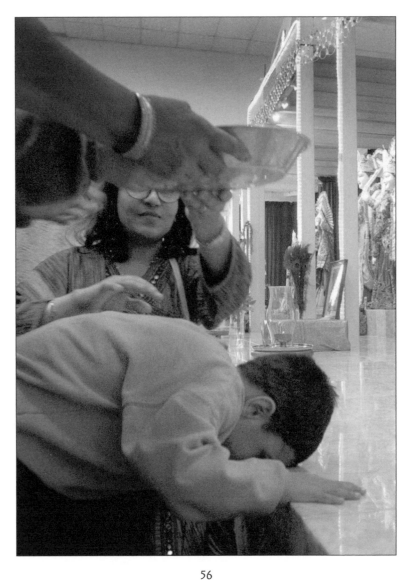

—3—

MOVING TOWARD DIALOGUE: FROM ISOLATION TO PARTNERSHIP

As Christians, it is important for us to be grounded in our own faith, with practices that keep us centered so we can face new questions, circumstances, and people. But once grounded, we need to assess where we are on the community journey from isolation to partnership.[24] As hosts and long-term residents of North America, we have power and prestige, and we make choices about how we relate.

- Do we isolate ourselves and exclude immigrants and refugees?
- Are we hostile and abrasive toward probable changes in our environment?
- Do we compete with the religions of new North Americans, trying to attract their adults and children into our faith community?
- Or can we partner and cooperate, even though we come from different perspectives? Are we open to being pleasantly surprised rather than threatened as we see our interests, practices, and theologies converge and diverge?

If we look at the history of our local communities and nations, we see the ways in which we have experienced and related to people of other faiths. Approaches include isolation from others, hostility toward others, competition with others, and partnership or hospitality.

A Christian who grows up in India has contact with other denominations within Christianity but also with Muslims, Hindus, Buddhists, and perhaps Sikhs and Jains. Friends and relatives may practice another faith and participate in various religious festivals and family events. The constitution of India guarantees freedom of religion in the midst of a pluralistic culture.

A Christian friend of mine from India reports that her Christian uncle married a Hindu woman. Their children have experienced both Christian and Hindu festivals, worship, and theology. They have attended Christian Sunday school and been baptized and confirmed. While in India and after moving to North America, the Hindu wife has continued in her religious practices, even as she regularly attends a Protestant church with her family and has raised her children as Christians. My friend reports on family members from India who continue to practice their faith, deepening their spirituality, while assisting children and spouses to practice a different religion.

My friend recalls many festivals and celebrations in India that were neighborhood events in which everyone participated. She herself went to a Christian elementary and high school in India, has a degree in theology from a North American seminary, and is active in her local Christian congregation and denomination. Her parents, who are second- and fourth-generation Christians, continue to be active in the Christian church in India.

She is frustrated with the intolerance of North Americans. "Do I want my children to be intolerant of others? Others are finding God through different paths, different religions. For many, it is their custom and their training. They have chosen or accepted their religion."

Her perspective is very different from many who have grown up in North America, where we are often raised in isolated Christian communities with few people of other faiths in our neighborhoods, families, or schools. Through reading, school, television, or travel we may hear, see, or meet members of other religions. But we absorb attitudes, stereotypes, and prejudices that we must examine if we are to move into more contact and conversation with peoples of other faiths.

It is important to become aware of our own selves and the issues that we bring to the discussion from our experience and background. We are not objective and may be unconsciously hostile. Movement into a multifaith neighborhood creates important theological questions and ethical dilemmas. We need to examine our own faith and beliefs, to reflect and adapt through attitude changes.

We will now explore isolation, hostility, competition, and partnership as responses to multifaith neighbors. We'll also look at power. Our multifaith neighbors see and know our power, even when we wish to ignore or deny it. We hold the important keys to creating a vibrant, multifaith society.

ISOLATION

Isolation can be geographic, cultural, or religious. Some characteristics of isolation include

- a clear consensus about the way things are and should be,
- accountability to God and the community itself, not to the outside world,
- a minimal knowledge of the larger world,
- a sense that this community knows the "truth" and a sense that others do not share this "truth" or this way of life, and
- no competition or hostility toward others, because they are dismissed as irrelevant to the member of the isolated community. [25]

Mennonite people[26] have experienced times of isolation because of persecution. They've sometimes chosen isolation for economic, educational, or religious reasons. Mennonite and Hutterite colonies have been established in Paraguay, Mexico, and Russia with few other people in their midst. In Russia, Catherine the Great and the Russian Orthodox Church asked German colonies, which were also Baptist, Lutheran, and Catholic, to limit interaction with Russian people so that the Russians would not convert from the Orthodox faith. Russian servants in some Mennonite homes were asked to leave while the family prayed. Then the servants came and ate with the family. Some German Christians would have had contact with various Russian Orthodox groups but were not to interact with them on religious or spiritual matters.

A humble superiority often resides in isolated groups because the others are more "worldly" and the group is "set apart" by tradition and choice. The isolation is reinforced through baptism, church discipline, and family ties. Little spiritual or faith conversation with others outside the community occurs, and it is not desired. Members of isolated communities may not wish to give a testimony about personal beliefs in Jesus Christ. Often they are attempting to replicate the early church by studying Scripture, worship, prayer, and mutual aid. Speaking the German language or a dialect keeps others at a distance, especially if the wider community speaks English, Spanish, or Russian.

Old Order Mennonite communities remain isolated even though they interact with other people. They have their discipline, lifestyle, and community, which they officially join at baptism. They are aware of other options but still choose isolation. Some may have experienced "worldly pursuits" before baptism but then decided to accept the isolation. Excommunication and judgment await those who are baptized and then leave the faith. An adult child leaving before baptism is less tragic for the Old Order family than his or her excommunication.

Hasidic Jews and other orthodox and conservative groups often remain in isolated communities, living in their own neighborhoods and interacting with other people only as necessary.

In some countries, a national religion is supported by the government in some way, and most people belong to it. Sweden's church is Lutheran, for example, while Portugal and Spain are Catholic countries.

When I work with men who grew up in rural Quebec prior to the 1960s, they speak of "Catholic" villages where the priest had the most education and was a civic as well as religious leader. Knowledge of other religions or Christian denominations was minimal. This changed significantly in the last half of the twentieth century, when many people stopped going to church and the clergy lost much of its power and influence. The environment became much more secular among vestiges of a Catholic culture.

Some traditions, such as Islam, are not as isolated as they are portrayed to be. Muslims respect Judaism and Christianity. Jews and Christians have lived in many Muslim towns and cities, which often hold synagogues and churches. Before 1948, approximately 150,000 Jews and many Christians lived peacefully in Iraq. Exodus from Iraq has primarily been a function of political struggles between Israel and many Arab countries.[27] Steady media portrayals of Muslims as fundamentalist and isolationist sometimes prevents honest analysis of the effects of Zionism, the British mandate, and western imperialism on the Middle East.

It is difficult to break into or break out of an isolated community. Coming into the community may mean learning many of the folkways and customs. Lifestyles and behaviors that have been learned from birth must sometimes be unlearned.

For many people in North America, globalization and shifting population patterns have reduced isolation. The United States is not the "Christian nation" that some claim it is. For instance, as we noted earlier, the 2000 census showed there are about the same number of Muslims in Illinois than United Methodists, about 350,000, but the number of Muslims is slightly higher.[28]

In Waterloo Region in 2001, the number of Muslims, Orthodox Christians,[29] and Pentecostals were each slightly more than nine thousand.[30] Growth has occurred among Muslims and other immigrant faith groups. The total number of Canadian Christians has increased less than 1 percent while non-Christians have increased by 72 percent between 1991 and 2001.[31]

In the United States, Christianity increased by 5 percent between 1990 and 2000, while Baha'i, Buddhist, Sikh, Hindu, Muslim, Native American, New Age, and Non-religious/Secular increase by more than 100 percent, many over 200 percent.[32] In Waterloo Region between 1996 and 2001, there was a 146 percent increase in Hindus, a 138 percent increase in Muslims, a 112 percent increase in Sikhs, and a 67 percent increase in Buddhists.[33] These increases are primarily due to immigration.

Immigrants to North America are often wrenched abruptly from their isolation by war. World War I, for example, changed the dynamics of many countries and groups. At the end of the war, national boundaries in parts of Europe and elsewhere were redrawn by the victorious powers. New countries were created as people of ethnic groups, faith communities, and cultures were thrown together under a single national banner. Sometimes a single ethnic group was disbursed among newly created entities. Countries were not divided along natural ethnic lines. For instance, ethnic Kurds became citizens of Iraq, Turkey, the Soviet Union, and Iran after the treaties of 1919.[34]

World War II and the Vietnam War also led to mass migrations. Refugees moved within their own countries and to new countries. This sometimes ended the isolation and ghettoization of people, but also created tension and hostility in their new homes.

HOSTILITY

A second response to other religions is hostility, which can occur when established communities see the newcomers as a threat. This fearful reaction to others can be used by politicians and other leaders to gain power. Negative forces sometimes energize individuals and groups who create an unsafe environment for those who are different.

According to Henri Nouwen, when people have their sense of security disturbed, they begin a "painful search for a hospitable place where life can be lived without fear and where community can be found."[35] In their search for community, immigrants often become victims of fear-filled hostility.

Roman Catholics and Protestants have viewed each other with antagonism at different times in different nations. Many issues that date to the Protestant Reformation remain causes of concern. Even in mid-twentieth-century America, parents lectured their children about dating members of the opposite faith. John F. Kennedy's election as president of the United States was an important breakthrough in overcoming stereotypes and prejudices against Catholics.

Extremist movements in some religions focus on the anger, resentment, and fear of people in the midst of change. For instance, *jihad* is defined as an internal spiritual struggle "against one's uncontrollable passions, lack of spiritual discipline, and tendencies toward illegitimate violence."[36] Yet it has been used by extremists to strike out against others in the name of purifying the world of evil. An inward spiritual discipline becomes a hostile outward action when interpreted by some leaders in a political context. There is no tolerance or respect when passions are exacerbated by some extremist leaders and by media that misrepresent faith traditions. Most religious adherents are tolerant and attempting to create communities of safety for all faiths.

Hostile speeches and comments toward other faiths by some Christians in North America has a very disconcerting effect on non-Christians who struggle for acceptance and are profoundly religious. As these remarks are reported in the media, recent immigrants do not know how prevalent this hostility is. They immigrated to become safe from oppression but now are fearful. Christians, who are more than 75 percent of the population in North America, may not realize how powerful these comments are.[37]

In *Moving Beyond Sectarianism* Joseph Liechty and Cecelia Clegg write about Northern Ireland. They see a "culture of blame" at work in the hostility of that land instead of individuals and leaders taking responsibility for their past and present actions.[38] Building hostility is much easier than the thoughtful reflection and action required to break the power of sectarianism, not only in Northern Ireland but in many other parts of the world.

R. Scott Appleby observes that religious leaders can work for positive and respectful social change or can be the force that augments hostility.[39] It takes the courage of someone like South Africa's Bishop Desmond Tutu to break the power of resentments and hostility so groups can learn to work together. How can religious leaders promote working together and healing rather than hostility and fear?

COMPETITION

Hindus, who believe in respect for all religions, sometimes view proselytizing as a hostile activity. Their interpretation has strong connections to British imperialism there, which supported a western missionary movement and brought many Western traditions to that country.

In North America, where competition is an accepted part of the culture, proselytizing is often viewed as a respectful offering of our faith in a context of partnership. North Americans are accustomed to churches competing to attract participants, somewhat like a business. Megachurches in particular are offering more and more service and activities with the hope of gaining members.

Many pastors, community workers, and mission workers strive to contextualize their ministry and respect the culture in which they are working and living. They often provide education, translation, healthcare, or other services when sharing their faith, living a testimony to the work of Christ. They can know the history of those they serve and be very careful, but they cannot determine their attitude or perspective. Non-Christians may still feel pressured to convert or to join a particular congregation, even when that pressure is not intended.

Competition is a far less destructive process than hostility toward other faith communities. Yet Henri Nouwen saw competition as a hostile activity. According to him, it fills safe places with preoccupations and activities that do not allow strangers to get to know each other. It does not permit freedom, but becomes a space filled with manipulation and noise. The community, which should be safe and free for all, begins to foist awards, promotions, exams, and grades on some, thus blocking hospitality. Through their religious leaders and committees, the hosts wield power and control, and force the stranger into the scheme. There is little room for the stranger to offer innovative contributions, explain other traditions, or relate his or her own experiences in other contexts or religions. Distance remains between the host and the stranger.[40]

Though competing religious groups often know each other well, there is a sense of strong sense of superiority toward the other. This makes it very difficult to communicate and to work together in matters that are not religious. For example, can they work together to build houses for Habitat for Humanity, sponsor refugees, talk with city governments about appropriate zoning for places of worship and meditation, or hold a community festival together? A sense of superiority opens a gulf between groups and can built resentment. They may not be hostile, but they do not accept each other.

Two characteristics of competition are

1. competing communities acknowledge that they have much in common, and
2. they both stress the differences and define their own superiority.[41]

Because superiority is stressed they are often unable to learn from each other or see each other's strengths. Thus dialogue and community action are difficult in the midst of competition, when differences are accentuated but not talked through.

Because competition is so deeply rooted in North American culture, it is an accepted aspect in the religious sector and appears "normal." It fills the emptiness and fear with noise and activity. We walk away from the angst, alienation, and estrangement that exists in the world and within each person. For example, after September 11, 2001, the United States has had an opportunity to explore its vulnerability and angst. Instead of struggling through the pain and fear, the president and government chose militarily action in Afghanistan and then Iraq. The noise of battle overcomes the voices of fear, anxiety, and loneliness. But underneath the noise, angst and spiritual longing for community continues throughout the world. The empty space is filled with mere activities and words.

Again, churches compete with each other for members. If we follow the example of megachurches, we seek to maintain good business practices, such as advertising, organizational design, meeting the needs of the members, being located near main thoroughfares or freeway exits, welcoming and greeting members and visitors, and so on. These practices are not inappropriate, but congregations should discern whether they compete with others or whether they cooperate and partner with them.

Gimmicks, business plans, and strategies for growth do not necessarily create hospitality, according to Nouwen's definition of it as friendship and freedom for the guest. Are guests taken into consideration when churches define their visions and goals? Hospitality offers a safe place, an empty space, where both guests and hosts can make their contributions without fear. It is a place where silence is honored.[42] The personal boundaries of both guest and host are not violated when they are in safe places.

Though the competition has subsided, the Council of Churches in Canada and the United States, along with the Evangelical Fellowship Canada and the National Association of Evangelicals have created a situation in which Christian denominations needed to decide which coalition they would join. A denomination could not be a member of both the evangelical organizations and the council organizations. Evangelical coalitions require members to affirm a doctrinal statement; the councils of churches are Trinitarian but have few other doctrinal affirmations.

Mennonites have members who feel comfortable in both the coalitions. How do Mennonites and other similar Christian denominations participate in both the council of churches and the evangelical coalition? For many years, Mennonite and others have been "associates," not voting or fully participating, but still attending both sets of meetings as observers. Competition is not neutral and does discriminate. It does not allow a safe space for all to make their contribution. Thankfully, these restrictions have change in Canada in the last five years and Mennonite Church Canada has been able to fully participate in both Canadian Council of Churches and Evangelical Fellowship Canada.

If we wish to have an authentic dialogue that leads to action, we must purge ourselves of the need to compete and to manipulate others. We must drop our need for success and power and become appropriately vulnerable. We must be prepared to listen—and we will certainly find times when we can speak.

EXAMINATION OF POWER

North American Christians have not addressed the power dynamic, which needs to be understood before there can be an authentic partnership. In North America, the culture has been determined by Judeo-Christian traditions. As newcomers ask questions about symbols and beliefs, especially in connection with politics and government, many citizens are offended and become angry. We do not realize the impact of religious values, Scriptures, and ideals on our governments. As hosts, we are in a position of power and may wish the guest to assimilate and to accept the current religious tenets in government, not realizing how difficult they are for the guest.

Currently the Ten Commandments are in the news in the United States. They have been called the basis of much law and a key ethical text for western societies. Wood and stone tablets of the commandments are in the chambers of the U.S. Supreme Court and are prominently displayed in many legislative buildings, schools, libraries, and parks. Some politicians are creating contention and forcing the courts or legislatures to make difficult decisions about the display of the Commandments. Politicians on both sides of the argument build up the insecurity and fear of many citizens, hoping that they will be reelected as the champions of their communities. Unfortunately they are setting the country up for an argument in which all sides will lose.

Many politicians believe in "limited power," that there is a definable amount of power in the world, and when one gains power, another must lose it. Therefore, if the Ten Commandments are removed, a group of people has lost power. An individual or group must work hard and use whatever strategies are necessary to keep their power. Hierarchy is often based on limited power.

In religious hierarchies, a person's power increases as they ascend to higher ranks. In religious organizations where power is centralized, local congregations may have less power over their buildings. Priests and pastors are guided by bishops or moderators, the congregation is expected to contribute a set amount to synod or diocese, and significant decisions are made either by chosen leaders or councils. The congregation may have power locally, but the stronger the hierarchy and the clearer the limited power, the fewer decisions are made at the local or congregational level. This illustration describes some Christian denominations, but I have also found other faith groups in which power is very hierarchical. For example, a Hindu temple may be governed by a guru in India. A priest or priestess is the guru's follower. Adherents have their local programs but are dedicated to the guru.

"Unlimited power" is an alternative concept that understands power as available to all people. It is power based in self-esteem and assertiveness. Each person can have power to maintain personal safety and assert herself or himself as responsible to make necessary decisions. Unlimited power is egalitarian. An individual possessing unlimited power can afford to be vulnerable and seek to understand the other person's situation and experiences. There is no need to win, and there is space to negotiate and to come to an agreement that is safe and acceptable to everyone. Everyone gains, and no one needs to win in a way that creates losers. The situation remains safe.

Many faith communities are "congregational," that is, much of the power resides in the local board or council. The national denomination, synod, or diocese receives its monies based on congregational decision. Congregations choose their pastors and leaders, and there may be some differences in theology and practice among the congregations. Each of the congregations is a respected member of the denomination or association.

Listening and speaking in a safe, empty space where different voices can be heard is essential. Playing a trump card and deciding the solution without listening is resorting to "limited power" and is abusive and manipulative.

North American Christians possess power in the multifaith conversation. Our first stance as people with power is to create a safe place where those from other faiths can explain their concerns, experiences, and beliefs. An attitude of respect and trust is essential. All participants must be seen as people of integrity.

This can be difficult because the newcomer of another faith may need to overcome stereotypes and preconceptions. We as Christians are unfairly branded—often by other Christians—with attitudes that we find repulsive and could never endorse. But it would be wrong for us to discuss all our personal beliefs in order to exonerate ourselves or differentiate ourselves from other Christians with whom we disagree. The other person will probably be bored and wonder if we are narcissistic, trying to convince them of our purity. A genuine attitude of vulnerability, acceptance, and humility will be more welcoming to the other person. It will indicate that we have opened our mind and heart and want to understand. Together with shared power and respect for each other, we find solutions and ways of working together.

After September 11, 2001, and after the invasion of Afghanistan, I called one of the Muslim imams in our region to indicate my concern for the safety and well being of him, his family, and his mosque. He replied, "We knew you Mennonites and staff at House of Friendship cared about us and worked with us. We were not in doubt of your friendship." He was remembering how we had worked together to obtain halal meat for Muslims using the House of Friendship emergency food hamper program. We had several sessions of Mennonite-Muslim dialogue. Two years before, the imam through Islamic Humanitarian Service along with volunteers from Mennonite Central Committee had been in Iraq delivering medicines and other relief supplies. We were all working together for a more peaceful world. Together we were partners with unlimited power.

PARTNERSHIP

Partnership can be entered into with neighbors from other faiths as we create the safe place where action and discussion can occur. The power imbalance is corrected or at least understood and acknowledged by the Christian. Even a simple statement of friendship, readiness to listen, and appropriate vulnerability sets the discussion on a positive note.

This partnership exists within the reign of God. Christians believe that God has significant relationships with them and with the Jews, but we do not know the many other ways in which God has been active in the world through other spiritual teachers, communities, and contexts. By starting with the Genesis narrative, we remember that God created all humans in the God's image because God has wanted friends. How has God moved among the many peoples who have been created in this divine image?

Our attentiveness and openness will help us to see the wider world of creation and God's actions. How does our neighbor perceive God present in the world? How does our neighbor love humanity and creation? How does our neighbor work to renew and restore this planet? How does our neighbor pray?

David Lochhead summarizes Karl Barth's questions that help ascertain if what we are hearing from a person of another faith conforms to the truths we already know.[43]

1. Does it cohere with Scriptures from the Old and New Testaments?
2. Is there continuity with the traditions of the church through history?

Can we evaluate the faith of our neighbor with "the fruits of the spirit" cited in Galatians 5:22? Can we understand the context from which our neighbor has come or is living? Does theology conform with action and behavior?

What effect does this conversation or action have on the Christian? As the Christian brings the experience to the congregation, how does the congregation evaluate the action or experience? Does the Christian and the congregation sense a call to repentance within the action or conversation? Do the individual and congregation sense the Spirit of God present in the action or conversation?

Is the conversation dialogical or monological? In a dialogical conversation, all parties are speaking and listening. Thus truth is found in mutual exploration. In a monological conversation, one party is speaking and the other party is listening; there is not a sense of partnership and mutual learning.

Several years ago, a leader from another religion attended a multifaith meeting. He was one of eight religious leaders from different traditions in the room. He did not ask whether we were familiar with his religion but talked continuously about himself and his faith. He monopolized the time together. I have had many positive experiences with other members of his faith, finding them deeply energizing and enriching. But this leader was not willing or able to enter conversation with us. He needed to control. We had other things on our agenda, but he ignored them. Still I listened actively.

Multifaith discussion and action cannot take place if a principal concern of the participants is conversion. Much monologue has occurred in this mode, and some individuals have converted. Nouwen's third spiritual movement—from illusion to prayer—is important here. If our purpose is conversion, we are operating out of the illusion of a sense of superiority about our faith. We are not respectful of the other person's experience. Nouwen encourages us to move from illusion to prayer, an active seeking of God's presence and concern for everyone involved. Action and discussion with our neighbors can be prayer, especially when we are working to sense the presence of God. God is present and active in the conversation; can we be silent, attentive, and open to this divine presence? We will want to listen for areas where we disagree, but not in a competitive or argumentative fashion. We may ask for clarification or for examples that illumine an issue. Listening is coming to the conversation not just to absorb, but also to reflect, digest, and discern.

Listening and being vulnerable provides opportunities to answer unexpected and important questions. IGR has spent four years discussing various theological issues with religious leaders who bring their faith perspectives to the table. As we discuss the agenda for the fifth year, members of non-Christian faiths are asking about the differences among Christian denominations. Each leader will give a half-hour summary of the origins and theology of their denomination.

These leaders from other religions need to understand the North American context. They are puzzled by the many denominations and want to know more about them. This opportunity to talk about denominations is not imposed but generates from their desire to know us more intimately because we are partners in IGR and in the community.

QUESTIONS FOR DISCUSSION AND REFLECTION

1. Have you experienced life in an isolated community, as described above? What were your reactions to the community and its members?

2. If a member of the Jehovah's Witnesses knocks on your door, how would you react? Is there much hostility in the experience? Is it a competitive encounter in which the denomination is trying to attract new members? Do you view that denomination as an isolated community?

3. In what ways is competition hostile, according to Nouwen and your experience?

4. Trying to persuade members of one church or denomination to join another has been called "sheep stealing." Do you feel that competition in the church is acceptable?

5. It is estimated that less that 5 percent of any population will change from one religion to another during their lifetime. Because denominational allegiance in North America is less strong, a larger number will change churches but will remain Christian. Should we compete for members? Should we partner with others?

A MULTIFAITH EXPERIENCE

Remember Abraham, Ishmael, and Isaac: The Festival of Sacrifice

The biblical figures of Abraham, Ishmael,[44] and Isaac appear in the Jewish, Christian, and Muslim scriptures and traditions. References to them occur throughout the Old and New Testaments, and the Qur'an. Interpretations of these three figures—a father and his two sons—have served as a way of divisiveness and a way toward peace.

My first awareness of the Qur'anic stories of Isaac and Ishmael was when the Muslim community in Waterloo Region celebrated Eid al-Adha (Festival of Sacrifice) at the end of the Hajj. The Hajj, or pilgrimage to Mecca, is one of the pillars of Islam. All who are able are required to make this pilgrimage at least once.

Muslims around the world celebrate Eid al-Adha as a way of joining with those who participated in the Hajj that year. Part of this celebration is to purchase a generous amount of meat (according to tradition, a whole goat, sheep, or camel). One third of the meat is kept for their family, one third for neighbors and friends, and one third for charity. Since the charity portion was donated to House of Friendship for use in the emergency food hamper program, I wanted to know the particulars of this festival.

In the Qur'an version of the story, Abraham was directed by Allah to sacrifice Ishmael, who was by then a youth in his early teens. (In the Old Testament, of course, it is Isaac whom Abraham was directed to slaughter.) Abraham experienced three visions from God with instructions to sacrifice the boy, who at the time was his only son. Abraham at first doubted these visions, but then understood that God was calling him. He said to Ishmael, "O my son, I see in a vision that I offer you in sacrifice. Now see what is your view" (Surah 37:102).

Ishmael was willing to submit to his father and to the will of God, saying, "O my father! Do as you are commanded. You will find me, if Allah so wills, patient and constant" (37:102). Abraham had Ishmael lay on the altar so that he could not see the young lad's face. Abraham's soul was crushed and his hand was paralyzed. He prepared to sacrifice his son, but the knife could not kill the boy. Allah instructed Abraham to sacrifice a ram, not Ishmael. This occurred near the Kabbal in Mecca, which is one reasons the festival is celebrated at the end of the Hajj.

The story as told in Genesis 22 parallels the one in the Qur'an, except that it is Isaac whom Abraham was told to sacrifice, not Ishmael. In Genesis, Abraham built the altar, put Isaac on it, and then was instructed to sacrifice a ram, not the boy. Abraham was declared righteous because he obeyed God and again received the promise that his descendants would be as numerous as the stars and the sands. His offspring would be a blessing for all nations.

These stories of Ishmael and Isaac lead me to examine the biblical narratives of Hagar and Ishmael. Hagar was the Egyptian slave of Abraham's beloved wife, Sarah, who was barren. She was eager for God's promise of "numerous" descendants to be fulfilled, so she decided to assist God by arranging for Hagar to have Abraham's son. Abraham was already eighty-six years old. Walter Brueggemann cites John Calvin's remark that Sarah's faith was defective.[45] Sarah constantly worked to help God. She offered Hagar to bear her son, then sixteen years later, she maneuvered to protect Isaac, who was not the first-born son of Abraham. Despite this maneuvering, God kept maintaining the covenant with Abraham and his offspring, but often not in ways that humans understand; the biblical characters God uses are not always ethical or attractive to us.[46]

Genesis 16 recounts the story of Ishmael's birth. After

Hagar became pregnant, the power dynamics between her and Sarah changed. A rivalry over who was most important to Abraham developed. Hagar could not take the pressure, so she left Abraham's family. God found her in the desert and asked her to return to the family. She received a blessing for herself and her unborn son. This was not the blessing of covenant—Isaac remained the main player in God's promise—but a vigorous assurance that Ishmael's offspring would also be a "multitude" (Gen 16:10). Hagar rejoiced that she had seen the face of God, who would protect and care for her. Ishmael was born after her return to Abraham's household.

The version of the story containing Ishmael's near-sacrifice does not appear in Genesis or anywhere else in the Old Testament, but only in the Qur'an. But we can view these as stories that tell about God's interaction with people, not as historical accounts. Ishmael was about thirteen years old when he was circumcised with all men as a sign that the covenant had been established (see Gen 17:23-27). He was therefore a full participant in the covenant. God blessed Ishmael and promised to make him a great nation, even though the covenant came through Isaac.

After Isaac was born, Sarah became jealous again (see Gen 21). She feared that the promise would pass to the oldest son, Ishmael. Abraham did not know what to do about the tension Sarah was creating in the household. God told Abraham to ask Hagar and Ishmael to leave. But God first assured Abraham that they would be all right. Hagar and Ishmael left with generous provisions. The Qur'an says Abraham provided dates, and took them near present-day Mecca. In both stories, Hagar and the youthful Ishmael almost perished until God intervened again and provided the water they need. In the Qur'an, a well appeared behind Ishmael. God's love for Ishmael continued throughout his life.

Rabbi Marc Gopin notes that there are legends that

Abraham, concerned about their welfare, later searched out Ishmael and Hagar to make arrangements for Ishmael's marriage.[47] Ishmael appeared when his twelve sons, promised by God, were named (Gen 25). When he died, Ishmael "was gathered to his people" (Gen 25:17). Gopin says that this phrase was used only for very important biblical leaders like Abraham, Isaac, Jacob, and others. Gopin wonders whether Ishmael is now with Abraham's people.[48]

Throughout the Ishmael story in Genesis, God and Abraham showed love and concern toward Ishmael and Hagar. Ishmael received all the blessings of Isaac, except the promise of the covenant.

Walter Brueggemann points out that God is not exclusively concerned about Abraham, Sarah, and Isaac. Divine attention and protection are also focused on troubled ones outside the promise. But "the very child who discloses the passion of God for the outsider is no small threat to the insider."[49] Eugene Roop notes, "Hagar and Ishmael have a future in the horizon of God."[50] God hears the cries of those who are troubled, oppressed, and suffering. Abraham cannot handle the tension in his own family, but God does not desert Hagar and Ishmael. They also have a blessing and protection.[51]

QUESTIONS FOR DISCUSSION AND REFLECTION

1. Do Christians and Jews remember God's blessing on Ishmael when thinking about Muslims? Ishmael represents the Hebrews' later fight to secure the "promised land" of Palestine. Do we need to interpret these texts differently in order to fully sense God's love of "insiders" and "outsiders"? If we see that Arabs, Jews, and Christians are equally significant and loved by God, do we have grounds for making peace rather than war?

2. Do the stories of Abraham, Ishmael, and Isaac provide a place to begin a new conversation among the three

Abrahamic traditions? Do the stories illuminate God's blessing and love as a way to peace and reconciliation?

3. Have we been too much like Sarah wanting to protect Isaac's birthright? Should we be taking our cues from Abraham and God, who are deeply devoted to both Ishmael and Isaac?

4. An interfaith discussion, especially among members of the three Abrahamic faiths, could begin with these stories in Genesis and the Qur'an. If we start with the premise that God loves everyone, do we find another route to peace with justice?

5. Brueggemann notes that Jesus' description of heaven as a house with many dwelling places (see John 14:2) suggests that there are rooms and mansions for Muslims and Jews as well as Christians in God's kingdom.[52] In light of this, how does our anticipation of life after death affect our work for peace and justice?

—4—

STRUGGLING TO BECOME NORTH AMERICAN: ENTERING A NEW WORLD

In North America, immigration since World War II has result-ed in growth in the number of people of non-Judeo-Christian faiths. Of the approximately four thousand Buddhists in Waterloo Region, Buddhist participants at Interfaith Grand River estimated that three thousand are new Canadians who have emigrated here since the Vietnam War and seven hundred are Canadians who have become Buddhist adherents. An examination of Canadian immigration statistics shows that as immigrants arrive in the country, they bring their faith with them. It is not surprising, then, that the growth in the practice of non-Christian faiths in Canada parallels the rates of immi-gration from countries where those faiths predominate. Buddhist temples and meditation centers have increased as more families have moved here from the Far East and Southeast Asia, for example. More mosques appear as immi-gration from Muslim-dominated cultures grows.

In *Canada's Religions*, Robert Choquette documents the growth in religions other than Christianity. While the Jewish population in Canada more than doubled between 1941 and 1971, the populations of Hindus, Muslims, and Sikhs were minute during that period. The number of Buddhists actually decreased by half in those years. But in 1991 all these religious groups each showed significant increases to more than 150,000 people in Canada. By 2001, Islam had more than doubled to well over a half-million adherents. The number of Hindus, Sikhs, and Buddhists doubled from 1991 to 2001.[53]

These increases resulted from changes to Canada's immigration policy in 1967 and 1978, as racial and religious discrimination decreased. Many new immigrants report significant prejudice throughout the immigration process and when they've gone to find work or when dealing with police, especially since September 11 when a number of Muslims and Sikhs in Southern Ontario reported personal threats and some violence to mosques. In community centers associated with House of Friendship, some mothers did not allow their children outside for several days and then again after the initial U.S. attacks in Afghanistan. Discrimination faced by people of color and of non-Christian faiths continues in subtle ways. Jeff Outhit in the *Kitchener-Waterloo Record* reports that most are satisfied with their lives but half the people surveyed reported some form of discrimination.[54]

There is plenty for Canadians and Americans to work together on so that all people are treated with respect and dignity, even as yet more people of color join our communities. Our awareness can help discrimination to decrease.

Statistics for Waterloo Region show steady growth in members of non-Christian faiths. The region also has attracted large numbers of immigrants, placing just behind the large cities of Toronto, Vancouver, and Montreal. The region attracts not only individuals and families just arriving in Canada, but also many who temporarily settle in another location before moving to the Waterloo area.

Other religions are growing faster as Christianity in the region remains relatively stable. The following chart shows the growth in populations of religions in Waterloo Region, com-

pared to the growth of the region itself, with numbers project-
ed to 2017.[55]

	1991	2001	2017
Region's population	374,325	426,400	509,600
Buddhists	2225	3700	4600
Hindus	2820	4200	7000
Jews	805	1000	3900
Muslims	3870	9300	21,900
Sikhs	1185	2600	4300
Other non-Christians	1045	1400	2100

Immigrants from Eastern Europe, especially the former
Yugoslavia, have brought their faiths with them, and Canada
has seen corresponding rises in Roman Catholic, Orthodox,
and Muslim populations.

Among Orthodox Christians, Canada's 1991 census
showed a population of 387,390. In the 2001 census,
Orthodox, the total was 433,835. In the Waterloo Region,
Orthodox have increased from 4,745 in 1991 to 9,370 in
2001.[56] The growth in the Orthodox population can be seen in
the increase in both the size and the number of churches and
community centers being built for Ukrainian, Russian, Serbian
and Greek Orthodox Christians. Coptic Orthodox from northern Africa are also increasing. Orthodox are Christian, but
might evoke the same negative response from Canadian
Christians as do adherents from other traditions.

Walking alongside these neighbors of other faiths from all
over the world requires a variety of sensitivities based on culture, language, religion, and country of origin. In the mid-
1990s, the Canadian Council of Churches initiated a program
in which Christians from different traditions could meet each
other. The Kitchener-Waterloo Council of Churches held two

evening seminars and invited leaders from various Christian expressions: Orthodox, Coptic, Korean, Hmong, Chinese, and others. Participants discussed the histories of their tradition, and many participants unlearned some long-held assumptions. A man from India was asked by one of the panelists when his family became Christian. He replied, "My family became Christian when St. Thomas came to India two thousand years ago." The exercise became a model for the Council of Churches' interfaith coalition.

∽

To demonstrate the differences among Canadian immigrants and to illustrate the struggles of immigrants, I will briefly describe some of the concerns and issues of Sikhs and Hmong. I have chosen these two groups because I have worked more extensively with the Hmong over the past twenty-seven years and with the Sikh for the past ten years. The Hmong are illustrative of a group in which many have converted to Christianity, while Sikhs have for the most part maintained their faith in Canada. It has been important for me to communicate and develop friendships with both these communities.

You might wish to imagine what you would experience if you moved to Punjab in India and suddenly lived in the midst of the Sikh culture, or if you emigrated to Laos and lived as a Hmong in the mountains.

Culture and religion are intricately mixed, so some questions and issues will be more cultural than religious. It should be noted that most Hmong are animist, but often become Christian after moving to Canada. The Sikhs, however, have maintained their faith and have established two Gurdwaras (centers for worship and community activity) in the region.

In 1902, five thousand Sikhs emigrated from India to Canada. Because of Canadian legal restrictions, only 1,016 were left in Canada by 1921. When Canada lifted the ban on immigrants from India, many Sikhs left during the sixties and seventies. Many professionals and businesspeople came for economic reasons. A number of Sikhs also went to the United States and settled on the West Coast.

In 2001, the Sikh population was 278,000 in Canada. They have established Gurdwaras primarily in British Columbia, Ontario, and Alberta, and have sustained active mutual aid systems. They have a good understanding of western-style democracies because they were governed by the British in India for many years. They are often fluent in English and Punjabi, and have done well economically. Most Sikhs emigrated to find better economic opportunities, or to join family and friends.[57]

In Canada, Sikhs face racial and religious prejudice and are subjected to ridicule and misunderstanding, especially if they practice Khalsa, because of their unique appearance. Many men find it difficult to obtain jobs while practicing Khalsa, so they cut their hair and cease wearing the turban.

Racial and religious prejudice increased in the 1980s and 1990s when a number of high-profile stories were reported in the Canadian press. One centered on the efforts of Sikhs to join the Royal Canadian Mounted Police but continue wearing turbans instead of uniform headgear. Another story was about conflicts that had developed between two groups of Sikhs in British Columbia. These were over the use of chairs in the Gurdwara worship area. (Sikhs traditionally sit on a carpeted floor to prevent class and income distinctions between worshippers.) Another story concerned some conservative Sikhs who were accused of blowing up an Air India plane. News media played up these stories without in-depth explanations of the religion and without portraying the peaceful and cooperative nature of most Canadian Sikhs. Cynthia Mahmood reports that all these incidents lowered the status of the Sikh community because of "the Sikh community's notable difficulties with public relations, but also the media's inability or unwillingness to penetrate the cultural, political, and religious complexities of Sikh life."[58]

The Hmong people with whom I've worked came from a mountain agricultural society in Southeast Asia. They've had a more difficult time adjusting to North America.[59] Hmong were forced to leave Laos because of their cooperation with the United States during the Vietnam War. Most Canadian Hmong were in refugee camps in Thailand for several years before being accepted into Canada, beginning in 1978. Mennonite congregations throughout Canada sponsored about five hundred Hmong refugees. Within five years, 90 percent had moved to Waterloo Region. They did not speak English and lacked the resources to start rebuilding their lives. They had little understanding of democracy. Their clans, organized by surnames, made major decisions corporately for all families in the clan.

Many of the Hmong women lacked education and were illiterate in their own language. They also found English very difficult to learn. The men who had been to public school knew Laotian and Hmong. Some had learned French and a few had learned English. The Hmong church pastor and volunteers took time to teach some women how to read Hmong so they could attend classes in English. Older women took care of children while younger women went to work. In their farming and hunting economy, parents had worked together in the fields unless the men had jobs or were part of the fighting in the Vietnam War. They were accustomed to living as extended families in one house. Once in Canada, most took jobs as unskilled workers. Fortunately two local companies hired many Hmong to sew and embroider. Working together and living close to each other provided necessary economic and social bonds, and many Hmong people were able to build financial capital.

A few Hmong were Christian, but most were animist. They needed herbs for healing according to their animist traditions.

They wanted to bury their dead near the place of birth or where ancestors could find the spirits of the recently deceased. They were concerned about good and evil spirits and were led by shamans. During this time of transition into Canadian life, many Hmong converted to Christianity. Their leaders received financial assistance from Mennonite Central Committee for a Hmong settlement counselor. The Mennonite Conference of Ontario and Quebec provided assistance for a pastor's salary, and the First Mennonite Church in Kitchener provided space for worship services, activities, and offices.

The Hmong leaders wanted to be like their sponsors and become Mennonite Christians. Mennonites were flattered, but wondered if the Hmong were converting only to please them. However, the Hmong church leaders felt strongly that Christianity overcame the fear and superstition of the animist faith. They were able to synthesize some aspects of traditional Hmong religion into their Christian practices. They also kept in contact with the Christian and Missionary Alliance, which published resources and held yearly retreats for Hmong pastors, church leaders, youth, and young adults.

For me, walking alongside Hmong was very different from walking alongside Sikhs, yet they have many issues in common:

- Parenting is difficult when children learn English and North American customs much faster than their parents do. At Hmong New Year's celebrations, older people wear traditional clothing. Youth and young adults wear western fashions. Some youth wear Hmong clothing, head dresses, and the family's ornate jewelry to perform traditional dances and then change back to North American clothes. At the Sikh Gurdwara, older members wear traditional Indian clothing while youth and young adults are in western clothing. Since all persons in the Gurdwara must have their heads covered, boys, and men wear the orange scarf on their heads unless they are wearing a turban, which is a long piece of cloth wrapped around their heads and covering their uncut hair. Some, but not all, of the men wearing turbans are Khalsa members. Women and girls wear a long scarf which covers the top of their hair and wraps around their neck. Since 2000, there appear to be more males wearing turbans at the local gurdwara as well as seen in public places.

Parents struggle to maintain discipline, teach traditions, and provide guidance to children heavily influenced by the North American culture. Children are immersed in the school system, but parents—especially older Hmong—are unfamiliar with the system and often lack the English skills to talk with teachers. Both Sikh and Hmong youth seem to do well in the school system, despite many challenges for their parents.

•Sikhs often arrange marriages for their children; sometimes the bride or groom comes from India. But second- and third-generation Sikhs are now choosing their own spouses. Since there are no clergy, the Gurdwara chooses spiritual leaders who are then recognized by the provincial government to perform weddings. Interreligious marriages between Sikh and Christians are often performed at both the Gurdwara and the Christian church.

When Hmong marry, the clan of the bride and groom set the dowry and negotiate arrangements for the wedding. Hmong rarely marry outside their community, but a number of Canadian Hmong have married American Hmong since no one is allowed to marry a person of the same clan. Negotiation between clans continues, with the clan leader advising the parents on the discussions. Five to ten days after negotiations are finished, the couple is married in a civil ceremony if they practice traditional Hmong religion or at the church if they are the

Christians. Most brides do not wearing the traditional Hmong garments but take to white wedding dresses, while men wear suits, and facilities are decorated in western decor.

• Sikhs continue to speak Punjabi in worship as well as at home. Children are taught the language and may go back to India to see family. Hmong conduct worship services in Hmong but increasingly need to have Sunday school classes in English because the youth and young adults' primary language is English. They can sing in Hmong and converse about household matters but are not able to discuss complicated subjects in Hmong. In younger Hmong families, very little Hmong is spoken other than formally at church. A young Hmong Bible college graduate was unable to lead services or preach to his congregation because he did not know enough Hmong, but he did an excellent job working with youth and young adults.

• Sikhs are more politically active than Hmong. Candidates for political office often visit the Gurdwaras and are invited to speak. Sikh delegations make appointments to meet with political leaders. A number of Sikhs have been elected to political office.

Hmong are less well known by politicians and community leaders because they are a small group. Working through Mennonite leaders and other friends, they have effectively dealt with political, community, and personal situations. In Laos, they are seen as a "backward people" and face discrimination. Before leaving Laos, some even changed their names in order to get into high schools and colleges.

• Both groups have family in their country of origin. Hmong also have some relatives in Thailand and in refugee camps. Sikhs are free to travel to India and visit. Hmong people have traveled to Thailand, and a few have gone to visit in Laos, but it is quite dangerous. If the government knows that a refugee has returned, it can create problems, even for those Hmong who have Canadian passports. Most Hmong settle for letters and the occasional telephone call back home.

•Hmong and Sikhs see themselves as Canadians, and most are citizens. Cynthia Mahmood writes that one young woman sees her nationality as Canadian, her ethnicity as Punjabi, and her religion as Sikh.[60] Hmong had visions of returning to Laos in the 1980s but are now entrenched in Canada. Though their children and grandchildren have been to Laos, they know little about their parents' lives there.

Some think of Sikhs and Hmong as being a diaspora. Sikhs originated in India and moved to Southeast Asia, Africa, Australia, Europe, and North America.[61] Hmong traditionally lived in mountainous regions in eastern China, but migrated south and eventually settled in Southeast Asia. Their practice of "slash and burn" kept families moving to new areas. After Hmong had planted crops for several years, the nutritional assets in the soil were depleted, and the families would move to another location and create a new village with fields and gardens. They would stay in this area until its soil became depleted. This method of agriculture kept them searching for productive land, but some Hmong remained in each region. Hmong now spoke various dialects of their language throughout the world. Instead of *diaspora*, some sociologists use the term "transnational" to describe groups now rooted in North America but having an ethnicity that connected them to a part of the world where they no longer lived.

Hmong and Sikh are two very different communities that have settled in North America for different reasons, with different cultures, and in different patterns. They are a small part of the complexity of "welcoming the stranger" and helping newcomers to be part of North American communities.

QUESTIONS FOR DISCUSSION AND REFLECTION

1. Imagine yourself as an illiterate Hmong woman moving to North America. You are an animist and worry about the spirits. You know how to protect your family members with herbs and other ingredients from mixtures from Southeast Asia. You do not understand the school or healthcare systems. How do you adjust? What do you do when your husband decides to become a Christian with the other members of his family?

2. You are a Sikh Khalsa man and have grown up wearing a turban. You come to North America to take a very good job. Do you stop wearing the turban and leave the Khalsa discipline? How do you deal with your loss of values and ideals?

3. Your teenage children are talking about a Sikh male child who is letting his hair grow. They say he has a kirpan, a ritual knife often dull and symbolic rather than sharp and carried by faithful males. The family lives in an upper-middle-class home and the parents are well respected in the neighborhood. The children are very good students and well behaved. What is your children's attitude toward the male youth? How do you respond?

4. Are there other families in your community who are struggling with North American values? How do you identify with them as you critique our culture and try to maintain Christian values?

5. How do you speak to people with different values and different religions? How do you speak to them so they understand your viewpoint? How do you listen or dis-

cuss without having to convert or change the other person? How do you build friendship and allow differences to exist? Have you observed and can you identify some differences that destroy friendship for you or others?

A MULTIFAITH EXPERIENCE

Cedar's Question: How Do You Read the Old Testament?

The following story was told to a group of pastors, sisters, scholars, and priests of which I was part at the Tantur Ecumenical Institute in Jerusalem. We were discussing the struggles of Palestinians and Jews is Israel/ Palestine. The story is recounted here from my notes of Cedar's testimony. My reason for being in Israel/Palestine was to study how Christians lived in a nation where they were in the minority, an estimated 2 percent of the population.

Cedar is the widow of an Anglican priest and an Arab Israeli citizen, living in Jerusalem, a city of Jews, Muslims, and Christians. Unfortunately very few Arabs and Jews live in the same neighborhood, but all faiths live in one city. She has come to a continuing-education class for clergy at Tantur Ecumenical Institute and asks how we read the Old Testament. For her and many other Palestinian Christians, it is difficult to read the Old Testament because they see themselves as descendants of Philistines and Canaanites. She daily observes the Israeli government's actions toward Palestinians, rooted in a theology that God has given them the land through covenant. Do Jews have a special relationship with God that means superiority? Do Christian claims that their religion is superior to others create destructive patterns for Muslims and Jews too? How do we read Scriptures and remember that God loves all peoples and that all are created in the image of God? How do we read of God's compassion for "insiders" and "outsiders" in all three Abrahamic faiths?

Cedar's family was forced to leave their home in Haifa in 1948 when the provisional Israeli forces captured many villages and expropriated the homes, businesses, and farms of Palestinians in many cities and towns. No financial reimbursement was provided. Palestinian families fled to friends in other areas, camped in fields, or took refuge in Lebanon and Jordan. Fortunately Cedar's family had friends in another city in Israel, so they left Haifa but stayed in the country. Her paternal grandparents went to Lebanon, fleeing Haifa by boat. They were never able to return. Cedar and her family never saw her grandparents again.[62]

Her family later visited Haifa and eventually saw their family home, but it was then the property of another family. Cedar was able to obtain an education and a teacher's certificate.

After her marriage, Cedar and her husband served several parishes, initially in areas with many Christians and later in a predominantly Muslim town in the West Bank. Before 1967, the West Bank was Jordanian territory, a difficult place for Cedar because of her fear that she and her family would lose their Israeli citizenship. Though she is Arab, Israeli citizenship gave her much freedom.

After incidents of violence, the Israeli Defense Forces would quarantine the people, forcing all residents to remain in their homes; this was done primarily in West Bank and Gaza. During one such military quarantine in her city, Cedar's teenage son needed to take his exams to go to the next grade in high school. The school was two miles away, and the trip was dangerous because Israeli soldiers patrolled the streets and alleys. Cedar and her husband pleaded with him not to go. But he was agile and determined to pass his school year. He said that he would use the back alleys.

As they were discussed the son going to his exams, Cedar's husband received a pastoral call. A family needed him to come because an older person was dying. He knew he must go. It was his duty as a priest.

In the early morning, both her son and husband left home.

Cedar worried and prayed all day. Her husband telephoned saying that he had arrived safely. He spent time with the family, stopped at several other Christian homes on his return, checking the streets before he ran to the next family's home. He arrived home before nightfall.

The son did not return for several more hours. He arrived home severely beaten. Israeli soldiers had caught him and said they did not believe that he needed to go to take his final exams. They beat him to obtain information he did not have. They detained him for the day and finally dropped him at the family's front door late at night. As he recalled his experience, he told his mother that he wanted to fight back but remembered years of learning the Christian story and witnessing his parents' own examples of nonviolence. Cedar was relieved because fighting back could have meant his death.

It took him several years to recover from his physical and emotional injuries, and he lost a year of high school credits. When an opportunity to move to North America for a university education and later a job came through, the son left Israel permanently. He married and remained in North America. Cedar's family needed to leave Israel if they wished to visit him, because he and his family cannot return.

After her husband died, Cedar learned that her Israeli citizenship had been revoked. It took her several years and significant legal assistance to regain citizenship. This brings her more freedom to travel and to volunteer for her church and the Sabeel Institute, a grassroots, Christian ecumenical organization that works at liberation theology for Palestinians through action and reflection. "Sabeel is Arabic for the way, channel, or spring of life giving water," that organization's purpose statement notes.[63] However, Cedar's children are only Palestinian.

As an Arab, Cedar daily faces obstacles and questioning. For generations, her family and that of her husband have lived in Israel. She asks whether the Jewish right to the land goes back to the Old Testament and the covenant with Abraham and Moses:

> How can I read the Old Testament and see Philistines, Canaanites, and other people in and near Israel be the villains? What happens to the sons and daughters of Ishmael and Esau? Are they not loved by God? Do they deserve the violence in Joshua and Judges as Hebrews occupy Palestine? I do not want God to abandon the Jews; they are also made in God's image. I would like everyone to live peaceably and justly in this land.[64]

Reading Old Testament books like Judges, Joshua, Samuel, Kings, and Chronicles are most difficult for Cedar. She does not know how to interpret them as a Palestinian. "Does God not care about the Egyptians who drowned in the Red Sea? Does God not care about us as we face continual loss of land and homes?"

Other Palestinians have left evangelical North American denominations and formed their own evangelical Christian church because their denomination supported Christian Zionism and dispensational theology. Palestinian Christians could not persuade their North American brothers and sisters to reexamine their biblical interpretation and theology. Huge gatherings of Christian Zionist tourists in Israel cheered former Prime Minister Ariel Sharon's speeches and military policies. They support Jewish settlers who grab more land from the Palestinian farmers. Christian Zionists hope that the apocalypse will come as Israel is completely settled by Jews. Many Israeli Jews, including those working with interfaith organizations, those against housing demolitions, and Rabbis for Human Rights, also feel very uncomfortable with the Christian Zionists.

A number of Palestinian Christian pastors have deep appreciation for the Old Testament. Several have significant training in Old Testament. Mitri Raheb and Naim Ateek[65] have written liberation theology books from Palestinian Christian viewpoint. They see both testaments demonstrating God's love and assisting them in finding liberation amid a very difficult political situation. They are also very aware of the Palestinian Christians' doubts and questions about the Old Testament. Sabeel Institute has now had several conferences with biblical and theological scholars refuting the base for dispensationalism and Christian Zionism.

As I have worked with the marginalized people and communities, the Old Testament, especially Exodus and the Prophets, have been very helpful and full of insight. Jesus' description of his mission in Luke 4 comes out of similar statements in Isaiah 61. His proclamation of the year of Jubilee is from Leviticus 25. Many of Jesus' teachings have direct references in the Old Testament. But in working with marginalized communities, I have often struggled with the institutions that keep people poor or oppressed. Do they have "hardened hearts"? Do they need marginalized people to maintain their status? Is the oppression subconscious? Can we transform or convert the offenders and oppressors?

We must continue to ask, Has our biblical interpretation forgotten the humanity of the people on the powerful side? Has it examined how God may be calling and working with the oppressor and the powerful to find justice and peace? Is there a sadness within God as the human freedom granted at creation allows people to persecute, kill, and destroy others? Certainly the Israelites struggle and suffer when they rely on themselves, worship other gods, or exclude the marginalized. But does their covenant with God give them the right to the land or to think of themselves as superior to other peoples? What about the texts that command them to treat sojourners and outsiders, even enemies, with respect?

Cedar experiences deep spiritual angst as she finds it impossible to read the profound and beautiful literature of the Old Testament. Yet she poignantly speaks of God's care and protection for herself and her family as they struggle in a very difficult political context.

QUESTIONS FOR DISCUSSION AND REFLECTION

1. How does your biblical interpretation and theological reflection consider the political and sociological? How does it consider God's involvement with oppressors and victims? How do you remember God's love for all peoples?
2. As I left for Israel, a rabbi friend said, "Brice, remember that the Jews fear annihilation." I remembered holocaust, pogroms, crusades, and other ways in which Christians felt themselves superior and inflicted harm on others. I also saw the oppression of Palestinians. How does biblical and theological reflection help us to find God's truth in this very difficult situation where Muslims, Jews, Christians, and Druze coexist on a tiny piece of land?
3. How do we speak to Christian Zionists and dispensationalists who are very supportive of the Israeli government's military actions? Do we distance ourselves from these Christian brothers and sisters? Do we speak the truth we know?
4. As we read and interpret the Bible, how can we walk with Cedar in her struggle with the Old Testament's violence against Philistines, Canaanites, and Egyptians? Does God take sides in battles and wars? How does God's compassion not extend to Israel's enemies?

—5—

SEEING OUR WORLD DIFFERENTLY: IMAGINING OTHERS' VIEWS

As we get to know newcomers to our community, it is helpful to imagine ourselves in their country of origin. What would we find difficult? Are there customs, behaviors, holidays, and lifestyle issues that are essential for us to live comfortably and keep our faith? After "walking in another's moccasins," we might begin to see our concerns with new eyes. Imagine yourself, for instance, as the only Christian in a culture that doesn't set aside a day of the week for religious observance and rest. How would you maintain faith practices structured around daily and weekly routines?

The book of Daniel describes issues the Hebrews faced in exile. The food was not kosher and the Sabbath was not observed. Hebrews were foreigners and slaves; another religion required their allegiance. They realized many would live the rest of their lives in this new culture. They hoped their children would succeed in civil service. Must they comply and eat repulsive foods? How would they survive without bowing to foreign gods? Daniel stood up to show that God was with him and his companions as they kept their Jewish faith and practices.

The difficulty for North American Christians is that we are often viewed as others saw the Babylonians in the book of Daniel.

- We eat all kinds of food and sometimes enjoy a rich diet.
- Our clothes are not necessarily modest by the standards of other religions; we give little evidence of our faith in our clothing.
- We have few public religious practices.
- We live in wealthy and powerful countries.
- We assume that our lifestyle and practices are superior; we don't understand why other cultures and religions do not want to imitate us.
- Others see us as very secular and question whether our religion is significant.

Imagine Daniel as a Muslim arriving in North America and trying to maintain his faith. In his motherland, he has the mosque where he can attend on Friday near noon. The mullah calls out over the mosque's speakers, and men make their way for prayers. Some women also attend in their special room; other women pray in their home, bowing toward Mecca on their prayer mat.

After arriving in North America, however, there will be no call from the imam when it is time for Friday prayers at the mosque. But he will want to be with other Muslims as they stand and kneel in devotion to Allah. Will he be granted time off at his job on Friday from 12:30 to 2:00 p.m. to go to the mosque?

Hindus, Buddhists, and Sikhs are surprised that Christians do not go to their churches more often. They often wonder why church doors are locked. Can a person not come and meditate or say prayers for a few minutes? Can he or she not bring an offering of food or money at midday or early evening? Why are there no clergy in the building during the week to lead prayers?

Devout Muslims pray five times a day. In countries where Islam dominates, these prayer times are part of the structure of the day. The imam calls people to prayer, and workers stop and go wash their hands, faces, and feet. They know the direction of Mecca in their homes and at their workplaces as they spread out their prayer rugs and pray.

Where does a Muslim pray at work in North America? He wants to wash himself before prayer. Public bathrooms are available, but he may be ridiculed if he washes his feet in the sink. Will people understand when he takes off his shoes and socks, then spreads his prayer rug on the office or factory floor two or three times during his working day?

People of other faiths wonder if North Americans are unfaithful, because they rarely pray in public. Sometimes they see people pray before eating in a restaurant, but generally the food is eaten without prayer when the waitress brings it.

Sikhs may wonder why people are not fed before they leave the church service. Their meals are prepared at the Gurdwara; they are not potlucks. There is always plenty of food in the Gurdwara, so no one leaves hungry. The Gurdwara is also a place of safety. Someone is always present at the Gurdwara, and anyone may enter at any time.

Muslims and Jews often need to go great distances to find halal or kosher foods. Their spiritual life is enriched and deepened by keeping their diet. A rabbi told me that it is difficult to live in a city with few Jews because there are no stores well stocked with kosher foods. This rabbi does not want to live in a Jewish ghetto but wants to follow his faith's dietary practices.

Jews and Muslims find it difficult to go to restaurants where pots, pans, grills, and other cookware may have contained or touched foods considered unclean. Many Orthodox Jews use separate dishes for cooking special foods. A restaurant in a large Jewish community or in Israel would follow these dietary patterns. Attending a banquet or other type of public meal is also problematic. Will there be a vegetarian option? Will the vegetarian food be served on dishes or prepared in bowls and pans that have been used for unclean foods? What additives were used?

Many North American Christians, unaware of these dietary difficulties and often afraid to ask about them, might simply avoid asking Orthodox Jews or Muslims to join them for a meal or even for dessert. But what message does this send?

Many Hindus, Sikhs, and Buddhists are vegetarian. They come into a Judeo-Christian culture in which meals are often planned around the meat dish. If invited to a meal or attending a banquet, many will choose to eat all dishes except those with meat. Some may not want to eat anything containing milk, cheese, or eggs, but there will be less concern over the cooking dishes.

What do non-Christians do during the Christmas and Easter holidays? Many participate in secular activities of the season and enjoy time off from work. Some non-Christian staff agree to work these holidays, hoping that allowances will be made for their own religious holidays.

During the religious holidays of other faiths, schools do not close, businesses remain open, factories keep producing, and professional services are expected. How can adherents to non-Christian faiths celebrate their religious holy days? These include Rosh Hashanah and Yom Kippur for Jews, Diwali for Hindus, Eid at the end of Ramadan or the Festival of Sacrifice for Muslims. Do workers have to use religious vacation days to celebrate their religious holidays? Are the children and youth excused from schools and activities, or are they declared absent? Do they not participate in their religious events, some of which last for two days. In larger cities, the worship and festive parts of the celebration are held in public arenas. North Americans are often invited to come to specific activities. The music, food, and language are traditional. Even though the hosts are willing to take time to translate and explain, will North Americans attend?

Modesty is a sign of religious devotion in many religions. Many faith groups request that arms and legs are covered by long-sleeve shirts and long pants or skirts. Sometimes robes are to be worn. When entering a synagogue, a Jewish man wears a yarmulke; in the Gurdwara, a Sikh man wears a scarf if he is not wearing a turban; in the mosque, many Muslim men wear a cap. In many traditions, women wear head coverings of some kind.

Some places of worship have separate doors for men and women to enter, and once inside, there are racks for shoes, which worshippers are expected to remove. Worshippers often sit on the floor unless they have flexibility problems and must use a chair. This may seem too ritualistic to some Christians, but people of other faiths may be puzzled when they walk into a church through a common door and sit together in the congregation. They may wonder why the sexes are not separated. It's good to remember that before the 1960s, many North American Christian women wore hats or coverings to church services. In some denominations, men and women sat separately. People would wear their "Sunday best." Many non-Christians are surprised at North American's informality in worship services.

In some faiths, it is forbidden for men and women who are not related to touch each other, especially in public. Sometimes a North American Christian may extend a hand to someone of the opposite sex, which can be embarrassing for both individuals. A similar situation would not occur with a Buddhist unless the person is a monk or nun. A polite bow is always an appropriate greeting. Often other Buddhists accompany the monk or nun because driving is forbidden them. These prohibitions allow the monk or nun to concentrate on spiritual tasks.

Some members of other faiths fear Christian proselytizing. They have seen how Christianity and western culture can be linked and have perceived Christian faith and western culture as a threat or at best a mixed blessing to their own religion and the culture of origin. Christian missions have often mixed western culture, business, medicine, and military as they've brought religion to non-western countries. Non-Christians struggle to assimilate with North American culture. They know they need to do so. But will North Americans be open to their values and allow them space to make the necessary transitions without losing the essence of their faith?

Trust can be built if North Americans take time to learn about other faiths and cultures. When people of faith share their convictions and talk about their practices in a non-threatening, noncoercive way, relationship and understanding develop. In the conversation, participants can compare and contrast. They can begin to check their assumptions about other religions. For instance, some North Americans may be surprised to find that within Buddhism are very different understandings of "higher power"; some Buddhists are atheistic, but still very devout. At the same time, the Buddhist may be surprised that the Mennonite Christian is pacifist, and a Jew may be surprised that the Seventh-day Adventist congregation worships on Saturday, the Sabbath. Conversations can compare ways of meditating or praying. As personal and family events such as marriage or the birth of children occur, different celebrations and meanings can be discussed.

Parents of other faiths may worry that their children will leave their own tradition and become secular or Christian. Sociologist Reginald Bibby reports that 6 percent of teens between fifteen and nineteen with Buddhist, Hindu, Muslim, or Sikh parents identify themselves as Protestant or Catholic. Fifteen percent of youth who have parents of these same faiths say that they have no religion at all.[66] Parents fear that their children, in order to find acceptance, will stop practicing their traditions. Some children leave the faith. Some immigrant parents reinterpret their faith and practices in forms more acceptable to North Americans. Some second and third generations reestablish practices that have been abandoned. After their family members resisted wearing the turban for a generation or two, Sikh men sometimes resume wearing it. Likewise, Muslim women often decide to wear hijab even though their mothers do not. Children also sometimes want to learn the language, music, and culture of their motherland.

The relationship of North Americans to their governments can be perplexing because there is often much Christian symbolism in official ceremonies. But totally secular government functions may not feel positive either. The taking of oaths by swearing on the Bible often makes no sense to people of non-Christian religions. Sikhs would be unable to use their scriptures for their citizenship ceremony, because their scriptures are kept at the Gurdwara. Muslims could not imagine using the Qur'an in this way. Some groups do not have scriptures that would be appropriate.

If we reverse the picture and place North Americans outside their home country, we can imagine that Christians living in a country where another faith predominates might struggle with the lack of Sunday observance. Businesses may be open seven days a week, as they are today in our western, secular culture, but Sunday hours in North America are often fewer than on the other six days. In Israel, schools operate Sunday through Thursday; workers are on the job Sunday through Friday noon. Does a worker take Sunday morning off each week to attend Christian worship? Do children go to school while the parents attend church? Does one need to send children to a Christian or expatriate school so that the family has Sunday as a day for worship?

When I was in Israel, I was at first confused when most activity stopped Friday noon; Saturday was the Sabbath. As we were going to church services on Sunday, other people were heading back to work, even at a non-profit organization, which rented office space on the campus of Tantur Ecumenical Institute, an education and renewal center of the Vatican.

One of the Arab Christian workers living at Tantur sent his children to the local public school on Sunday while he and his wife went to church services. I wondered what I would have done: Sent my children to Christian school? Gone to church without my children? Tried to find church services on Saturday? Sought out occasions and programs other than Sunday worship for my children to learn about the Christian faith? Worshipped with my children at home? Used a home Bible-study course for children and youth?

The rector of Tantur Ecumenical Institute often told people who called him on Sunday, "I did not call you on Friday and Saturday because I respected your Sabbath. Please do not call me on Sunday." He respected Muslims' practice of going to prayer Friday noon or early evening as well.

Holiday seasons such as Christmas and Easter also present problems for North Americans in countries where these two holidays are not celebrated. Does a person take vacation time from work? At Tantur, American Thanksgiving was celebrated, and others were invited to a turkey dinner at noon. Residents kept to normal schedules in the morning while staff prepared the feast. It was a wonderful holiday afternoon occasion. But others needed to go back to work because it was not an official holiday. A similar experience occurred at Christmas and Easter, when Christians needed to step outside the public schedule. In Israel, Passover often coincides with Holy Week, which makes this an easier celebration. But the usual schedule resumes as Christians celebrate the resurrection on Easter Sunday.

In many countries, western dress is unacceptable. Long sleeves, long skirts and pants, and head coverings are expected, especially for women. People have to adapt, even though they wish for less clothing in hot weather.

North Americans are fortunate that they can be hosted and eat with any family that invites them. But it may be difficult to invite guests to the North American home, especially if the guests are from different traditions.

Women in North America enjoy significant freedom and may view women in other cultures as repressed. Some cultures are patriarchal while others have found ways to maintain the dignity of women and girls. I sometimes wonder if we bring our own biases to how feminism is implemented. Can a woman who is wearing a hajib be feminist? At one Muslim conference, the imam recognized a question from the male side of the curtain and then a question from the female side of the curtain. How many North American conferences have women asking as many questions as men?

Some women have appreciated the respect and safety that special clothing and separation have given them. Others want to have more freedom in the public sector.

In Iran and some other Muslim countries, many women have obtained an education and are doctors, professors, lawyers, and teachers. On the other hand, there are no female imams. Only Conservative and Reform Jews ordain female rabbis. Buddhist nuns have a much lower status than monks. Equal rights and opportunities for women are not universally accepted. Tradition still holds in many cultures and is often an issue when people come to North America.

North American women gained many of the rights and privileges they enjoy only after long, difficult struggles. We must remember that the status of women varies in other religions and cultures.

We can again use the book of Daniel as a metaphor for the experience of the foreigner who seeks to maintain his faith in a strange land. Daniel was a young man when he was exiled to Babylon. He refused to give up his religious practices, even under the strong pressure of King Nebuchadnezzar and his court.

A Jewish diaspora was scattered throughout the world until the 1950s, when many emigrated to Israel. From the apostle Paul's missionary journeys, we see Jewish settlements around the Mediterranean in regular contact with Jerusalem. To what extent were these Jews ghettoized? Do they assimilate the Roman and Greek cultures, though they kept Hebrew alive in worship and had schools for their children?

The Jews were persecuted before and after the Roman Empire became Christian. Many Christians find pogroms, or any persecution, repulsive. This oppression demonstrated the continuation of the risks that Daniel faced in Babylon.

So how do we now make room for all religions? This is a struggle for all people of faith. It is important to see how we are viewed as we seek to walk in the shoes of others and imagine their struggles.

Imagining is a first step. Studying the history of other faiths is also important. Then we need to take the risk and meet our multifaith neighbors. They can tell us their stories. If we take the time and prepare, we will hear all sides of their experiences.

QUESTIONS FOR DISCUSSION AND REFLECTION

1. North Americans are often depicted as wealthier and less moral than people who come from countries where non-Christian religions dominate. How are comparisons to the biblical Babylonian uncomfortable for you as a North American Christian?

2. How is it helpful to think of immigrants and refugees as Daniel and the exiled Israelites trying to maintain their faith amid pressure to assimilate to Babylonian culture?

3. Are we willing to make room and celebrate more holidays if there are a significant number of persons practicing a certain religion in our community? How do you handle your discomfort or anxiety?

4. Imagine yourself in a third-world culture with a mission and service organization. You need to adapt to many of the customs and set aside much of your North American lifestyle. What would trouble you most?

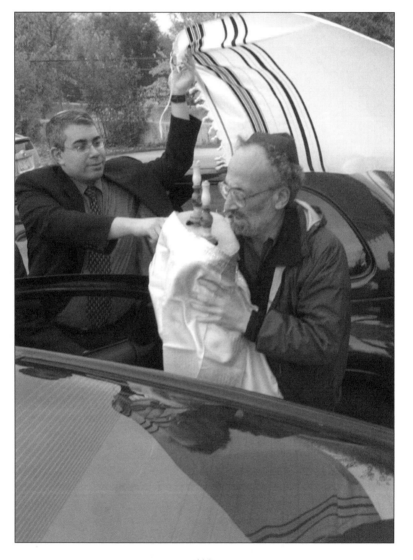

—6—

CAN WE BECOME A MULTIFAITH SOCIETY?

ATTENDING THE OPENING OF PROVINCIAL PARLIAMENT

Through my work with Interfaith Social Assistance Reform Coalition (ISARC), I came to know many Members of the Provincial Parliament (called MPPs) and to know their faith traditions as well as their party affiliations and positions on social issues. Public sessions were primarily political and dealt with current policies, but occasionally there were private discussions in which an MPP expressed the importance of faith in decision making.

After a recent election, the opposition party came to power. I was invited as the guest of the local MPP to attend the opening of the Ontario Provincial Parliament. A brass ensemble from the university played marches and classical music as the audience and legislators assembled. The whole ceremony was rooted in British and Anglican traditions. Honorary military officials brought in the flags and ushered in the speaker of the house and the lieutenant governor, who represents the Queen of England in ceremonial occasions. It was very formal, traditional, and elegant. Additional chairs were placed in the aisle and along both sides of the clerks' area for dignitaries, including representatives from the Roman Catholic Church, the

Anglican Church, the United Church of Canada, and the Salvation Army.

During the service, the speaker of the house led the audience in the Lord's Prayer. Other portions of the litany referred to Jesus Christ.

I felt awkward and uncomfortable. The service reminded me of seeing flights of stairs when I worked at the Independent Living Centre, an advocacy and personal support program for the physically challenged. I had wondered, "How does a wheelchair go up stairs?" I felt I had traveled back in time a hundred years.

At the ceremony in parliament, I was surrounded by MPPs from many different traditions—Jewish, Sikh, Muslim, Christian, and Hindu. Others practiced no religion. So why is the province conducting this service and celebration with traditional Christian prayers, and symbols? Census statistics indicate a growing non-Christian population. Why aren't all the peoples and religions of Ontario respected and recognized at this important occasion?

Like most Christians, I am usually pleased to see the acknowledgment of my faith in the public sector. But I am equally offended when people of other faiths need to keep quiet or acquiesce as their own traditions are ignored in a public celebration ostensibly for all people of a community.

Douglas John Hall wrote that we are moving out of the era in which Christianity held its traditional authoritarian role to a postmodern era that is "highly critical of religion and increasingly secular in its assumptions."[67] Though Christianity is obviously the "official" religion of our North American culture, there are signs that it is declining in influence. Many try to tell its triumphal story of ongoing success rather than working toward a radical assessment of the place of Christianity and all religions in our society and our government.[68]

In 1986, ISARC began at the invitation of a government

commission that realized how much charitable activity the faith community was doing for vulnerable people. The commission wanted a critique of their reform of social assistance. ISARC responded and continued to advocate on behalf of the economically and socially marginalized in Ontario. Based in faith communities at the provincial level, ISARC spoke out about social policy, laws, regulations, and procedures. It talked with legislators and government staff about hunger, homelessness, children's needs, disabilities, affordable housing, refugees, and many other issues. ISARC provided educational events for religious and community leaders, congregations, synagogues, temples, and mosques. It provided analysis of how programs affected communities and marginalized people. And it brought a moral and ethical voice to the discussions.

Previously some religious leaders from large denominations had gone to the politicians to affect changes at the provincial level by expressing the moral authority of their constituent base. Some religious leaders in ISARC hoped to use the same style and techniques. But in the mid-1990s, the premier of the province did not see the need to talk with a delegation of religious leaders. Setting an appointment to meet with him took two years.

Some of ISARC's religious groups expect little recognition from the government. They have not gained much power and have not had the ear of "the establishment." Mennonites, Sikhs, Unitarians, and Jews do not expect politicians and governments to listen. Those of us from these traditions carry a legacy of persecution and minority status.

Leaders in mainstream denominations have often been invited to meet regularly with government leaders. But newcomers from other faiths hold no power in their new countries. Discussion at the ISARC board has helped us all theologically and practically as we adjust to a new era in the relationship of religion and government.

Douglas Hall would ask Christian leaders to intentionally disestablish Christendom and disengage from the privileges of Christianity. He maintains that Christians can still push for moral authenticity, work toward meaningful community life, uphold the transcendent and mysterious aspects of life and spirituality, and discover and uncover the essentials for meaningful life as individuals and communities.[69]

Corporately the religious community has less power than other sectors and is often discounted. The political sector is disestablishing not only Christianity but all religion for a number of reasons:

1. Canadian politicians realize that members do not follow religious leaders to the polls. In Canada, religious leaders rarely recommend a politician to their membership. They are more likely to speak about issues addressed by the political parties and about questions to ask candidates. Catholic bishops have asked their members to vote based on political parties' positions on gay marriage, homosexual rights, and abortion issues. These requests have not always been followed by the membership. If religious organizations speak out, they highlight issues, rather than individual politicians. Politicians rarely appear at religious services, even during an election campaign.

   In the United States, some Protestant and Catholic leaders are strongly encouraging their members to vote for particular candidates. Candidates sometimes appear in churches, and some Christian organizations allow their membership rolls to be used by political campaigns. The organizations encourage their members to vote one way or the other. These developments are being debated within the denominations and in the public forum. Media analysis of President Bush's victories in

2000 and 2004 are said to be partially due to a heavy turnout of evangelical Christians, seemingly offering evangelical Protestants a stronger voice in national politics.

2. Religions are ambiguous, according to R. Scott Appleby, and "religions are powerful medicine."[70] There are peacemakers and terrorists in all religions. All have fundamentalists and liberals. Religions and religious leaders are often unpredictable. Governments find it difficult to discern which segment of the religious community they are meeting.

3. With religious pluralism, political leaders often do not know how to work with all the groups. They are afraid they will discriminate against some, so they steer clear of all.

4. Politicians express frustration at the number of coalitions of religious groups. They don't know who to contact or who speaks for the faith communities. There is no hierarchy or even agreement among the ecumenical and multifaith coalitions. The religious sector can be confusing for politicians who want to hear one voice.

On the personal level, many politicians are active in their faith communities, receiving their education in religious schools and attending worship on a regular basis. Prime Minister Pierre Trudeau was educated by Jesuits and attended Catholic mass regularly, becoming even more devout after his retirement. Much of his political ideology has roots in Catholic social teaching. But publicly he was silent about his faith while prime minister.

Former Prime Minister Joe Clark presented a lecture in September 2002 at St. Jerome's University College on the topic of the connection between the religious and political sectors in Canada. When questioned by students about his personal faith and how it impacted his decisions, he refused to answer. Yet as the audience entered the hall, a local Catholic group distributed pamphlets condemning Clark for his pro-choice stand on abortion. The bishop of his electoral district in Alberta asked priests there not to offer him the Eucharist because he was pro-choice. Yet Clark continues to be an active Catholic. His policies, especially those in the 1980s, when he was Minister for External Affairs, had a strong social justice slant, very much a result of his Catholic training and faith.

Rev. David Pfrimmer, ISARC chairperson from 1986 to 2004, worked on social policy issues for the Evangelical Lutheran Church in Canada. His doctoral thesis surveyed federal and provincial politicians and found that many had entered politics because of their religious ideals and values. They hoped to make positive changes in the nation and the province. They said they would appreciate more discussions with religious leaders and theologians of their own faith community and multifaith coalitions to talk about ethics and values as they review legislation and debate issues in their caucuses. But neither the politicians nor the religious leaders found the right forum for these discussions, away from media attention.

When Ontario Premier David Peterson came to Kitchener in the mid-1980s for a breakfast meeting with area leaders, he applauded local MPP John Sweeney. "We are about to make a decision at the provincial cabinet," Peterson said. "And John Sweeney will say, 'I have an ethical question I would like to raise before we vote on this decision.' John's question and the ensuing comments always make a significant impact on the final vote."

Moral and ethical questions are important in political discussion and for individual politicians. Politicians expect the faith community to come to the table with rigid positions rather than unique perspectives and questions. Can we find forums where these issues can be discussed openly?

QUESTIONS FOR DISCUSSION AND REFLECTION

1. Have you ever been to a legislative session of a government body, such as a city council, or a state or provincial assembly? How do you see the dominance of Christianity at these sessions? How would you imagine how a Muslim, Buddhist, Sikh, Jew, or Hindu might feel at such an event?

2. How much influence should the religious sector have in government and politics? Have you ever discussed your political perspective with another Christian or with someone from another religion?

3. How does the media represent your faith community? Is this representation accurate?

4. In the news, terrorism is often connected to Islam. What is your impression of Islam? Do you find that reporters are well informed?

—7—

BEGINNING WITH LOVE

Neighborliness is the positive friendship Jesus used to embrace all people in the world. Loving our neighbor as ourselves is a cornerstone of our faith and, as Jesus tells us, the second greatest commandment. In that passage, a lawyer tested Jesus, asking him which commandment is the greatest. Jesus responded, " 'You shall love the Lord your God with all your heart, and with all your soul, and with all your mind.' This is the greatest and first commandment. And a second is like it, 'You shall love your neighbor as yourself.' On these two commandments hang all the law and the prophets" (Matt 22:37-40).

This formula is not new. We are commanded in Deuteronomy 6:5 to love the Lord. Jesus refers to Leviticus 19:18 when he summons us to love our neighbor as ourselves. Micah 6:8 provides a similar synthesis when it asks, "What does the LORD require of you but to do justice, and to love kindness, and to walk humbly with your God?" These passages make clear connections between the love of God and our attitude and behavior toward other humans.

The book of James engages in the debate between faith and works (see James 2:14-26). James addressed questions that had emerged in the fledgling church. He was clear that our actions indicate our faith. Christians may talk about faith, but they will be judged by their actions. James' teachings echo others from the Torah and the Gospel of Matthew, especially the Sermon on the Mount (Matt 5–7).

James used the examples of Abraham, who because of his faith was willing to sacrifice Isaac, and Rahab, who practiced hospitality to her enemies, the Hebrews, by helping them into the walled city and then hiding them (see James 2). Rahab also is recognized in the genealogy of Jesus because of her courage and love. We remember Abraham also as hospitable to strangers who turned out to be angels.[71]

Enemies and strangers are our neighbors. Loving neighbors is an important practice throughout the Bible. Believers in the early church were urged to demonstrate their faith through love. In the parable of the Good Samaritan (see Luke 10:25-37), a lawyer questioned by Jesus about the essence of the law gave the appropriate response: to love God and neighbor. But the lawyer also had a question: "Who is my neighbor?" Jesus expanded conventional beliefs by making the Samaritan, the despised outsider, the one who helps the victim in the story. Jesus and the lawyer would have been aware of the unmentioned prejudices against Samaritans. Jews did not speak to or interact with them because their faith was viewed as a distortion of proper Judaism. The prejudice against Samaritans was so strong that the young man could not even say "Samaritan" after the parable, but had to say, "the one who showed him mercy."[72] We often miss how shocking Jesus' story was for Jews and Samaritans of the day.

The lawyer knew that Jesus' parable conformed to the Torah. Strangers and sojourners might practice a different faith, perhaps even worshipping idols, but they were to be respected while they live among the people of Israel. The lawyer was caught between cultural prejudice and the principles of love in the Torah.

Our neighbor is not only the person just like us, with whom we are comfortable. Our neighbor is the stranger, the sojourner, the one who is different or may frustrate us. Jesus takes us on a journey to meet our neighbor, not just the one who responds to our kindness, but everyone in the community.

Jean Vanier asks who we see as our friends and neighbors. Do we allow marginalized individuals and families to be our friends? Do we allow ourselves to receive wisdom from them?[73] Or do we see ourselves only as providers and helpers, lacking the expectation that they have some important gifts for us.

The parable of the Good Samaritan has always held significance for me in my work with economically and socially marginalized people. Pursuing my vocation as a community pastor has led me to people of diverse lifestyles, perspectives, economic statuses, and backgrounds. As I meet each new person, I first recognize the "image of God" embedded in them, as it is within myself and everyone else I know. As I learn to know and work with these men and women, this image of God becomes manifest and transcends all categories and differences between us. As I listen to their experiences, a trust and friendship based on respect and our common humanity is created by God.

Paul said that love is more important than our achievements. It is what endures forever: "We see in a mirror, dimly, but then we will see face to face. Now I know only in part; then I will know fully, even as I have been fully known" (1 Cor 13:12). His love for God pushed him to love all other people, even though imperfect. Marcus Borg describes being "born again" as our becoming more open and closer to God, which challenges us to see love as a gift. Our growth in love and compassion is a gift we will want to exercise.[74] We are not loving by ourselves but are experiencing God's power within us as we reach out and love our neighbors. We cannot experience God's gifts for us until we welcome, love, and engage everyone as neighbor. We may ask later, "What was I so afraid to risk? Why did I not allow God's grace to move through me? Why was I so hesitant?" Until we reach out, we will not see the God's image in others.

In Vanier's experience with L'Arche, a community of developmentally delayed and physically challenged people, he finds wisdom and beauty among individuals. He and Nouwen lived in L'Arche homes with other residents, many of whom had been previously institutionalized. Nouwen often took L'Arche residents with him on speaking appointments in Toronto. The residents were integrated and loved, and their gifts were recognized even though others in the audience or setting may have felt uncomfortable.

☙

Recently the topic of *sharia* was discussed at Interfaith Grand River (IGR). Sharia is Islamic law as derived from the Qur'an. Some countries use civil authority to enforce it. Many in the discussion automatically discounted the value and usefulness of sharia. They based their views on accounts by western media in countries such as Nigeria, Iran, and Saudi Arabia. Feminists in the group were particularly disturbed by the male domination in societies governed by sharia and reports of women being abused and sometimes killed by male religious leaders.

At the time, sharia was a hot topic in Canada because the Ontario government had produced a report by a former MPP who was an ardent feminist. Her report indicated that sharia could be the basis of an arbitration strategy in family conflict among Muslims, though it would still need to conform to the human-rights code and Canadian law. Arbitration would mean that the decisions of the imams would have the weight of the law and would need to be enforced by the courts. For example, if a husband decided to divorce his wife and the case went to religious arbitration, the imam's decision on the divorce would have the force of law. Licensed religious leaders might also have the right to decide custody of children, financial settlements, and alimony. Since licensed religious leaders in Ontario can officiate at marriages among members of their congregation or mosque, some argued that they should also be able to decide other family legal matters. Those opposed to the arbitration plan were concerned that women could lose some rights in this process.

After the initial discussion at our IGR meeting, a Buddhist participant e-mailed all the members an editorial on sharia. In a series of follow-up e-mails, a feminist, neopagan IGR member debated the issue with a conservative Muslim man who had worked for the local Shi'a mosque. Their conversation was broadened by a Reform Jew, who had read the Ontario report and knew the author. He made several significant points about other religions that have family courts and arbitration processes. He summarized the limits to sharia as determined in the report.

The IGR participants expressed surprise that this debate could be carried on in a rational and respectful manner. The participants in the e-mail exchange witnessed their views changing as they experienced respect from each other. The Buddhist had wondered whether he was acting responsibly when he started the debate. The neopagan stated that she normally would have rejected the conservative Muslim's "male opinion," but she responded to his e-mails and learned from his forthright and honest comments. Both respected each other and removed many barriers to conversation. There was no consensus, but there was understanding and openness to the others' wisdom. They had become respectful and listening neighbors.

Christian, Hindu, and Sikh members of the group affirmed that the debate had helped all of us. The steering committee decided to work on a process to educate the larger community on sharia, which was being used by some groups to marginalize and stereotype Muslims in Ontario, even though most disagreed on sharia as a method for family mediation in Ontario.

As the committee reviewed this process, all were pleased that individuals with divergent opinions and religions could respectfully work with each other and that the work ultimately began a process to assist the larger community to become better neighbors.

Christians are called to love and respect all as neighbor, and all neighbors no matter their faith. All of us are made in God's image. In our neighborhood, wisdom, truth, and creativity will yield gifts when we respectfully listen, ask questions, and meet each other. As hosts, Christians have a responsibility to reach out and extend the hand of friendship.

∽

What are some practical ways of beginning and continuing to understand the neighbor and his or her religion? We need to begin somewhere. Like the lawyer talking with Jesus, we know that our salvation and our deepening faith in God is linked to our ability to reach out to the neighbor who is different.

First, we must accept that multifaith neighbors have different personalities. Some will be attractive to us, but others less so. As good neighbors, we need to be open and reflective. Are the reasons for our hesitation based on personality, religion, culture, or appearance? Are some of these reasons superficial? We are hosts who may have lived for many years in an isolated Christian community. We might need to stretch ourselves, be patient, learn more, and then risk in order for friendship to develop.

It is important that we learn to know our neighbors' names. If they are new to North America, we should try to learn their names as they would say them in their homeland. Many immigrants Anglicize their names to better fit in. When my wife worked at a retail store, the employees began talking about their names at a social occasion. All who were new Canadians had changed their names in some way so that others would find their names easier to pronounce or spell. While working among Chinese, I have found that many have taken a new name or simplified their name for Canadians. It is an important sign of acceptance to ask a person for the name they have been given at birth and then work at learning their real names. Some may prefer an Anglicized name and we need to respect this choice.

Second, we can find ways to welcome them into the community. Taking food products—such as home-baked goods or garden produce—is a traditional welcome. If the food is vegetarian and has no preservatives, this is generally acceptable. But it is important to let the neighbor know exactly what the food is. We may wish to take an item unique to the region or helpful in all homes, such as pretty kitchen towels.

Third, we can be attentive without being nosey about the family's celebrations, changes, or concerns. We can loan items the family may not yet have, such as a lawn mower or a snow shovel. Is there a new baby? Are there guests for a period of time? Do the children want to walk to school with our children? Do they know where businesses and stores are located, especially good quality stores with reasonable prices? Or, if there is an older person in the home, are they aware of senior citizen programs in the area? These are some of the ways we can be helpful to newly arrived immigrants.

Below are some long-term commitments that prepare us to meet our multifaith neighbors.

READING AND LEARNING

As we are befriending newcomers, we can learn about their religion and their culture. Again, there are many resources at libraries and on websites. We may even want to read some novels about people, religions, and places where our neighbors have lived. For instance, *The Kite Runner* by Khaled Hosseini is an excellent, absorbing novel about a father and son from Afghanistan and their move to North America.

Television specials may feature the religion of our neighbor.

Documentaries or movies about the religion can be borrowed or rented. These may be generalized, but they can help us begin to see differences from our own North American and Christian cultures.

I have also been greatly helped by Christian priests and theologians who have lived in third world country with a non-Christian religious group. They find convergence in meditation, beliefs, theology, and principles of each religion, while acknowledging the divergences between the two. For instance, Aloysius Pieris writes in a Buddhist context; Swami Abhishiktananda in a Hindu one; and Kenneth Cragg in a Muslim one. All have remained faithful Christians, are significant leaders in their denomination, and yet are learning practices and theology from the other religion.

ATTENDING FESTIVALS AND CELEBRATIONS

I am surprised how graciously I am received when attending festivals, special events, or lectures sponsored by other religious groups. Some of their leaders and members know me from activities in the region. They want to be able to host me and take time to explain the importance of various symbols, foods, clothing, music, liturgy, and architecture.

When attending a Christian or Anglo event, I remain somewhat anonymous. When attending the service or activity of another faith, I sometimes stand out. I therefore prepare myself by alerting a neighbor or friend in that group that I will be present. He or she might be embarrassed if I were there without being hosted and without personal greetings. My friend may also be involved in the activity and make a conscious effort to greet me.

We know the most important days for all Christians, but we can expand our awareness of Christian festivals celebrated by the Orthodox and of holidays of other religions. Every year I buy a calendar that mark the important dates of various religions in Canada. It usually lists some cursory information about the day. At House of Friendship, we have purchased these calendars so staff will be aware of holidays and important times. I use a highlighter to indicate days that are significant for our neighbors and community participants.

Recently we planned a summer retreat for an interfaith organization, but it turned out to be on a Jewish holiday. The Jewish members politely excused themselves from attending, and I regretted not having the calendar with us during the planning.

All religions value family celebrations. Again, you can be aware of festivals through an interfaith calendar. Knowledge of your newer neighbors' celebrations can be a good conversation starter. When an invitation comes to participate at a community or family event, ask for more information and anticipate responding positively after checking with the rest of your family or others who you are responsible to. If you cannot attend, be direct and express regret. Do not leave your neighbor wondering if it is a real commitment or reticence and apprehension. Conversation with your neighbor can include questions about dress, foods, activities, meaning, and history. You can also ask if this festival is celebrated in the same way in all cultures of the religion.

When attending these events, try to relax and socialize. This can be difficult when you are so obviously different from others, but your neighbors will assist you to act appropriately. There may be unfamiliar and awkward times, but a welcoming neighbor will expect and sometimes anticipate your discomfort. Ask what is expected. Some uncomfortable times may occur if you are asked to do something like go to the front of the line when receiving food. You will probably be introduced and treated as a special guest. You may struggle with your own embarrassment or discomfort, but you'll maintain your humility if you remember how important your attendance is to your new neighbors.

Though worship is open to the general public, it is important to ask about protocol if you are going to visit a house of worship. For example, you may need to enter through a special door, wear a head covering, or remove your shoes. If worshippers sit on the floor, older or disabled people can usually get chairs.

You likely will not be expected to participate. When I visit a mosque, I sit at the back of the room. I do not know the prayer routine or understand Arabic. It is actually inappropriate for me to participate since I am not Muslim. I take time myself to meditate while observing. When the imam gives the sermon, it is usually in English. During the time of extended prayer, my host will join the other men or women standing shoulder to shoulder. At the end of the prayer, I talk with neighbors and others both inside the main room, as I am putting on my shoes, and then in the parking lot before traveling home.

In a Sikh Gurdwara, all men, women, and children enter by the same door and then proceed to take off their shoes and put on the scarf or something to cover the hair if they are not wearing a turban or scarf already. All go into the main room and sit together on the floor, with men and women on different sides of the room. The singing of the scripture continues in the Punjab language. After the service, you are expected to have a vegetarian meal with others. At this meal, people sit in rows and are not separated by gender. Plates, utensils, and food are brought to each person. There is time to talk with neighbors during and after the meal.

Hindus do not separate by gender or remove shoes at worship. Guests would be expected to stay for a vegetarian meal.

Regular worship and festivals are usually in the places of worship. Neighbors might invite you to their homes for special meals, such as Eid at the end of Ramadan or during the Festival of Sacrifice. Jews might invite you for the Sabbath meal after Friday-evening worship. You can talk with your neighbor about going to mosque, temple, or synagogue before coming to their house for the meal. Let your neighbor help you make that decision. Taking a gift for the host is acceptable, but do not ask to "bring something for the meal," because most foods for special events are family or culturally determined.

The music, dancing, and activities at worship and festivals will not be North American. You may not enjoy it, but be tolerant. It is an educational experience. An appropriate response might be, "I've never heard this music before, and I need time to understand it."

KEEPING ABREAST OF THE WORLD NEWS

Neighbors will be thankful if you are aware of news in their country of origin. There is often limited news of other countries in local newspapers or on television, so you might ask the neighbors how they follow news in their country of origin and whether this news is available in English. You can also check news on websites. Following are some good news sources.

- Holy Land Trust operates the Palestinian News Service, which brings regular reports from West Bank, Gaza, and other parts of Palestine. Israel has several good newspapers with websites: the *Jerusalem Post* and *Al Harretz*.
- The BBC and other cable news channels have websites that offer world news.
- CNN has operations in other parts of the world that carry a different perspective. My son and I have both listened to CNN London, which reports more world news than the American arm and often reports American news with a different perspective.

The press is not free of bias, and it is important to try to sense biases when reading or watching the news. Biases are often determined by the outlet's ownership or traditional associations. Once bias can be identified, it is a little easier to maintain some objectivity. Especially when there is a conflict in a particular area, you may want to try to obtain news from several perspectives.

The news can often lead to conversation. Expatriates will often check the news in their native language through the Internet. When discussing issues, it is important to listen, ask questions, and be open to what others are saying. You do not have to agree, but it is helpful to keep an open mind. You may want to include others of that religion or country in the discussion. There is diversity of opinion in every country, just as is in North America.

Many mission, service, and religious organizations maintain websites with stories from places where they are active. Christian Peacemaker Teams, for example, offers news provided by their personnel in locations where they are working. You can also find background and opinion pieces on these sites, giving another side of the news delivered by mainstream outlets.

CONNECTING WITH INTERFAITH ORGANIZATIONS

The number of interfaith organizations is growing, and most have websites. The Pluralism Project at Harvard University lists over five hundred of them in the United States. The United Kingdom has 140 organizations, with 43 percent of them founded since 2000.[75] Canada also has many interfaith organizations operating in major cities. Unfortunately many have small budgets and receive limited coverage in local media. Some are not even listed in telephone directories. Many of them can be discovered through networking.

It is worth the effort to locate interfaith organizations operating in your community. You can then keep in contact through their newsletters, through websites, or through a representative from your congregation or denomination. You might wish to encourage your pastor to participate and ask your congregation to support interfaith activities.

Some interfaith organizations hold educational activities that bring together people of different faiths. In Waterloo Region, Encounter: World Religions works with IGR to hold seminars in which participants learn about major religions. IGR then works with local congregations, temples, mosques, Gurdwaras, and synagogues to arrange for seminar participants to attend worship or prayer services.

Increasingly religious organizations are setting up dialogue sessions involving faith leaders to discuss worship, spiritual care, theology, world events, and history. Check your own denomination to look for resources.

One resource for a Sunday school class or adult study group that takes this approach is *A Muslim and a Christian in Dialogue* by Badru D. Kateregga and David W. Shenk (Herald Press, 1997). Each chapter includes essays on a topic, written from both Christian and Muslim perspectives. This would also be a good book for Muslims and Christians to discuss together. The Methodist Church in the United Kingdom has developed "The Life We Share," an interfaith study course with video materials and booklets.[76] More and more materials like these are being produced in the English-speaking world.

Christians learn about other religions when they serve on church committees that sponsor refugees. When a local congregation asked me to talk to them about religion and culture in Afghanistan, I invited an Afghan man who works for House of Friendship and has been living in Canada for five years. He discussed his experiences, his Muslim faith, and his family. He helped listeners understand some of the issues facing refugees of the past decade and explained some of the confusion they encounter upon arrival in Canada. All committee members were thankful for a forum in which they could ask questions of someone with first-hand knowledge of what new arrivals face.

TRAVELING FOR LEARNING

Many North Americans are able to travel and find interesting tours in countries where their neighbors came from. This is a wonderful way to learn about a religion. You can see its significant sites, observe worship, learn the history, see daily life, and taste the foods while experiencing the music, art, dance, and architecture of the land. Just being part of a faith's weekly schedule can be eye opening. In Jerusalem, for example, the Sabbath begins on Friday evening and extends all day Saturday. The weekend ends at sun down on Saturday evening. On Sunday morning when Christians are normally going to worship, most people are headed back to work. Christianity still is an important ingredient in the area, but only 2 percent of the population is Christian.

Travel agents may not always know of tours with a specific focus on learning about the religion and culture of an area, but you can also check with church and multicultural organizations. As you learn to know your neighbors better, you may find opportunities to travel with them or allow them to assist you in making plans and arrangements if you visit their country of origin. Most will have books or other resources which will help you understand the people, customs, places of interest, and foods you will encounter.

VOLUNTEERING

You also can volunteer in local organizations that assist immigrants and refugees. There are sometimes opportunities to work alongside traditional agencies or governmental departments that operate community centers in multifaith neighborhoods. School boards and other agencies are often looking for volunteers to help teach English as a second language, which is a good way to help others and to learn about religion and culture.

The House of Friendship operates four community centers and an emergency food hamper program, with participants and volunteers from different religions and cultures. Christian volunteers can develop trusting relationships while helping immigrants adjust to their new surroundings.

Schools with multifaith populations need volunteers. Helping parents participate at the school can be vital as they settle into their new homes and try to support their families. Children learning North American culture are often practicing the religion and culture of their parents' homelands. They connect very easily and can be bridges between families with diverse religious and cultural backgrounds. They are very observant and will probably be eager to learn about North America. We can encourage them to teach us some things about their religion and culture and make a special effort to meet their parents. This may not be easy for people without their own children around, but it is one way to connect that is often overlooked.

CONCLUSION

Welcoming a neighbor might feel awkward and uncomfortable at first. We might be hesitant and uneasy. But we are the hosts in our country and neighborhood. We are the ones who need to reach out and begin the process of building friendships. We will make mistakes, as will our neighbors, so we need a sense of humor.

It helps to find others we can talk with about our experiences, especially people familiar with the multifaith context.

As with the church committee that learned from an Afghan refugee whom another church had sponsored, we need to open ourselves to a giving and receiving relationship in which we will be host *and* guest. The gifts of the Spirit await us in these loving relationships. It might not be what we expect; we need to relinquish control of how the events unfold. But we can allow ourselves to see more clearly through the glass as we proceed in love. God is with us, helping us to receive divine and human gifts.

The process of moving toward a multifaith society is not easy in North America. We feel the loss of important symbols as Christianity awkwardly disestablishes. For example, prayers and Bible passages may not be used in civil ceremonies. The ceremony may seem very secular. At other times, scriptures from many religions may be used. Our North American culture is filled with Christian symbolism; our neighbors may ask about sayings, customs, or practices which we assume are normal, but would not be known or understood in another country. While in Israel, the city workers were putting up the electric light symbols for Hanukkah; when I flew back through London and then to Canada on December 17, many symbols of the season were Christian in origin. Many of us who are engaged in meeting our multifaith neighbors are concentrating on making this continent a safe and hospitable place for all. This will be most rewarding and energizing. We will be changed. We will discover God's presence among us, within ourselves, and in the neighbor. God is with us into this new future.

There are practical and attitudinal ways to prepare ourselves for this journey. With God and our neighbor, we create a community of peace, justice, respect, and generosity. Our decision is to begin.

As our neighbors become more diverse in the faiths they practice, Christians are reminded of the two greatest commandments:

•Love God.
•Love our neighbors as ourselves.

The two cannot be separated. All of humanity is our neighbor, made in the image of God. Our first response to our multifaith neighbors is love.

QUESTIONS FOR DISCUSSION AND REFLECTION

1. The Scriptures are very clear about loving our neighbor as an extension of loving God. Can you recall times when this has been difficult for you? Can you describe a time when you have loved others and were questioned by fellow Christians?

2. Is it difficult to find God's image in people? How do you see the divine light in each individual?

3. What do you fear about a future in which Christianity is disestablished? What do you find hopeful about such a future?

4. What are your next steps in meeting your multifaith neighbors?

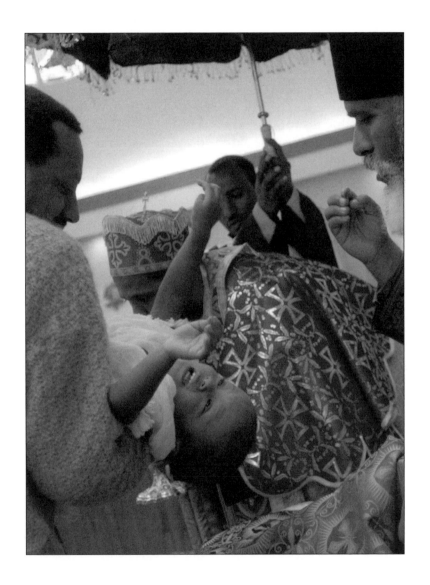

AFTERWORD

Gurdwara. Ramadan. Diwali. Yarmulka. Khalsa. These religious customs and expressions are unknown by many, if not most, North Americans. Yet they are part of the religious and cultural landscape of our neighborhoods. They are important features of the identity and practice of many of the new immigrants to the continent. In this text, Brice Balmer provides a helpful introduction to encounters with the religious practices and cultural observances of these immigrants. He offers a handy resource to help North Americans gain some understanding of the faith of our new neighbors. The information he provides is, however, only incidental to his real purpose.

Balmer has at least three primary purposes in this text. First, he wants to alert us to the growing presence of people of other faiths who are our near neighbors. The evidence he puts forth is incontrovertible. Second, he wants to encourage a compassionate Christian response to this growing phenomenon of increased religious diversity in our neighborhoods. Third, he seeks to provide some orientation and guidelines to equip Christians for the encounter with our multifaith neighbors.

As a very important subtext, Balmer is also seeking to undo the intolerant, disrespecting, and often violent response by Christians to diversity. Compelling his impassioned plea for tolerance is an inventory of memories of the ways in which Christians too often have dealt with people of other faiths and cultural backgrounds. Hovering in this territory are the historical memories of the Crusades, the Inquisition, the Holocaust, the Middle Passage, generations of slavery, the Trail of Tears, and the internment of U.S. Japanese during World War II, among others. Balmer is scandalized that these atrocities are closely connected with the Christian story. Can we write a different story this time? His eager commitment to a more hopeful saga fuels the passion in this text.

Balmer draws on the biblical text to highlight the Christian imperative to welcome the stranger and alien among us. He powerfully demonstrates our call to be people of generosity and compassion. He invites, encourages, and coaxes us to see hospitality as a faithful and necessary Christian response to our neighbors. Maybe we can get it right this time. At least this is his heartfelt hope.

But he is not satisfied to merely articulate a vision and express this hope. Balmer uses personal stories of the ecumenical experiences in the multifaith community where he works. He cites biblical injunctions to build bridges to our neighbors of multifaith backgrounds. He supplies exhaustive information from cultural practice and religious observance to break down stereotypes between people of various faiths who now share the same space.

Balmer's plea cannot be timelier. The current tensions between Muslims and the "Christian" West in the winter of 2006 have exploded into violence all across the Islamic world, fueling an increased threat of terrorism by radical fanatics within Islam. For many in the West, including many Christians, the issue that gave birth to this violence is framed in terms of an ultimate value: freedom of speech. For most Muslims, on the other hand, there can be no greater value than respect and reverence for the prophet Mohammed. At issue in the outpouring of violence and rage is a failure of understanding. What is clearly needed is encounter and dialogue that is respectful and seeks to understand. We need more voices like Balmer's that call us to disavow narrow tribalisms and the kind of bigotry that breeds suspicion and hostility. I sincerely hope that Balmer's message will reach a large audience and that his vision will be embraced.

In the encounter between Christians and people of other faiths, the question that needs to be answered is, "What does it mean to be a follower of Jesus in a multifaith society?" What is our faithful Christian response as members of a society that is characterized by religious pluralism, ethnic diversity, and cultural relativism? Balmer does not ask, and therefore does not answer, the question that many Christians would ask: Should a Christian's encounter with neighbors of other faiths focus solely on dialogue or should evangelism be a part of the engagement?

Within the Christian community are at least three common variants of what constitutes a faithful response to our multi-faith neighbors. First, there are those whose bigotry would not allow them to even consider people of other faiths as neighbors. If they had the power they would like to ship these people back to where they came from. Some Christians see little use for engaging these neighbors in dialogue except to identify the flaws in their religious constructs and to discover ways to refute them. The only point of any engagement is to convert these neighbors before they go to hell.

We can be thankful that for most Christians this response is not even an option.

Second are the Christians for whom a primary value is tolerance and respect for people of other faiths. Many of this persuasion base their posture of tolerance on a belief that all religions ultimately lead to God.

At opposite ends of the spectrum these two types of Christians, usually labeled conservative and liberal, often line up either in support of engagement solely for the sake of conversion or for tolerant engagement that does not countenance the possibility of conversion.

Balmer leans strongly in the direction of those that regard tolerance as the primary virtue. Ashamed of the sometimes sordid history of Christian engagement with those who are different, he implies that the highest Christian value is that which will avert the possibility of repeating that history. He pleads for tolerance. To be sure, Balmer's grounding in the biblical narrative issues in a call for more than mere tolerance. He sees the Christian imperative requiring a response of welcome and hospitality, dialogue, compassion, bridge building, and understanding.

However much I affirmed and cheered Balmer's exhortation, I found myself wanting to ask him whether this was all we were called to in relation to our non-Christian neighbors. I wished that Balmer would at least grapple with whether tolerance, hospitality and welcome represented an adequate fulfillment of our calling vis-à-vis our non-Christian neighbors. I found myself struggling with the question, "Is there another way between these two poles of conversion without respect and tolerance without conversion?"

I wish that Balmer would have located the foundations for our response to our non-Christian neighbors in the purposes of God. He alludes in the text to a negative spirituality from his experience of working with alcoholics. We learn that this is a spirituality born out of shame because of abuse. He notes that the shamed person is often angry, resentful, and frustrated, and that behaviors are often reactive. It seems quite probable that the commitment to tolerance is a response to the attitudes of ignorance, arrogance, disrespect, and actions born of hostility that issue in violence of which we do need to repent.

Undoubtedly the purposes of God encompass everything that Balmer would include as imperative for a truly Christian response: generosity, hospitality, welcome, respect. There is,

however, in the biblical text another stream that is not necessarily a contradictory one. Particularly in Luke's gospel, Jesus
seemed to always link compassionate response to the poor, the
broken, the hurting, and the suffering with an unapologetic,
even enthusiastic, announcement of the reign of God. This
announcement invites a response (cf. Luke 4:18-19; 7:18-23;
10:1-16). In his letters to the Ephesians and the Colossians,
Paul wrote of the cosmic, all-encompassing scope of God's
redemptive purposes in Jesus Christ.

> [Jesus] is the image of the invisible God, the firstborn of all
> creation; for in him all things in heaven and on earth were
> created, things visible and invisible, whether thrones or
> dominions or rulers or powers—all things have been created
> through him and for him. He himself is before all things, and
> in him all things hold together. He is the head of the body,
> the church; he is the beginning, the firstborn from the dead,
> so that he might come to have first place in everything. For
> in him all the fullness of God was pleased to dwell, and
> through him God was pleased to reconcile to himself all
> things, whether on earth or in heaven, by making peace
> through the blood of his cross. (Col 1:15-20)

And again,

> With all wisdom and insight he has made known to us the
> mystery of his will, according to his good pleasure that he set
> forth in Christ, as a plan for the fullness of time, to gather up
> all things in him, things in heaven and things on earth.
> (Eph 1:8b-10)

We are not called to judge whether those who are not
Christians are outside the scope of the grace of God. Indeed the
Christian church has made enormous strides away from an
arrogant posture that in the past condemned all non-Christians
to hell. For many centuries the theology of St. Augustine

inspired western Christians to believe that those outside the church are damned. At the Second Vatican Council, however, Roman Catholics moved from the posture of *extra ecclesiam nulla alus* (outside the Church, no salvation) to a more humbly generous posture. They found themselves willing to affirm that "the Catholic Church rejects nothing of what is true and holy in other religions." Indeed, some Catholic theologians, such as like Karl Rahner, began to speak of "anonymous Christians" and allowed for the possibility that devotees of non-Christian religions could be seen as "implicit believers." Hans Kung, another Catholic theologian, made the observation that other-than-Christian religions may provide an "ordinary" means of salvation. By contrast, the Christian gospel provides an "extraordinary" means of salvation.

Even Protestant evangelical theologians and practitioners have for some time been moving away from a blatant rejection of every element of non-Christian religions. Don Richardson, author of *Eternity in Their Hearts*, posits that God has revealed himself to more people than we might imagine. He postulates that the one invisible God is resident in many folk religions. Christianity doesn't replace this revelation, he says, but completes it.

Given this greater openness to allow that God's revelation is not confined solely to the Christian faith, does this mean that tolerance and dialogue are the all-encompassing scope of our mandate? Kung has written that, in spite of the tragic failures of the Christian church reflected in our bloody and ignominious history of inhumanity toward those of other faiths and cultures, bearing a positive and uncompromising witness to the uniqueness of our Lord, in his life, death, and resurrection in all aspects of our evangelistic work, including interfaith dialogue, is of the essence of what it means to be a follower of Jesus Christ.[77]

While we cannot judge the end for those who are outside of

Christ, the Bible seems to call us to a witness "in bold humility," as author David Bosch says, to Jesus Christ as the embod-
iment of the purposes of God. Lesslie Newbigin captures this
spirit in his articulation of the character of the Christian's witness and conviction.

> It has become customary to classify views on the relation of
> Christianity to the world religions as either pluralist, exclu-
> sivist, or inclusivist. . . . [My] position is exclusivist in the
> sense that it affirms the unique truth of the revelation in
> Jesus Christ, but it is not exclusivist in the sense of denying
> the possibility of the salvation of the non-Christian. It is
> inclusivist in the sense that it refuses to limit the saving grace
> of God to the members of the Christian church, but it rejects
> the inclusivism which regards the non-Christian religions as
> vehicles of salvation. It is pluralist in the sense of acknowl-
> edging the gracious work of God in the lives of all human
> beings, but it rejects a pluralism which denies the uniqueness
> and decisiveness of what God has done in Jesus Christ.[78]

After his return from India Newbigin was troubled by the
cultural relativism of the West and the focus in the ecumenical
churches in the West on interchurch aid. The incipient danger
Newbigin saw was that this approach would strip the gospel of
its central claim about the work of Christ. It would remove
from the churches their obligation to proclaim Christ in worship, preaching, prayer, service, and witness to the kingdom of
God. Newbigin felt the World Council of Churches was risking
its own life and integrity in jettisoning the obligation to proclaim God's finished work in Christ.

Newbigin rejected as an abstraction the question about
whether the non-Christian could be saved—that is, whether the
non-Christian would go to heaven after death. That determination was God's alone to make. In addition, Newbigin asserted
that

there is something deeply repulsive in the attitude, sometimes found among Christians, which makes only grudging acknowledgment of the faith, the godliness, and the nobility to be found in the lives of non-Christians. Even more repulsive is the idea that in order to communicate the gospel to them one must, as it were, ferret out their hidden sins, show that their goodness is not so good after all, as a precondition for presenting the offer of grace in Christ.[79]

In his own life Newbigin demonstrated an earnest commitment to sincere dialogue with non-Christians. This does not detract, however, from the call to bear witness to Jesus with these persons of other faiths. Newbigin remarked that Christians share the human story equally with non-Christians. He further observed that we make decisions about the part we will play in that story, decisions we cannot make without regard to others who share that story. That shared commitment, he commented, is the context for true dialogue. This dialogue is not about sharing religious experience. Nor is it about who is or is not going to be saved. While it may include that consideration, the dialogue is essentially about the meaning and goal of the human story. It is Newbigin's conviction that in the dialogue Christians must tell the story of Jesus, the story of the Bible, as the power of God for salvation.

Despite my reservations about what I believe is a fairly serious omission, Balmer's treatise is not only timely but also urgent if we are to avoid the tragedies that have weighed so heavily on the history of the Christian movement. I hope that members of congregations all across North America will read this book, learn about our neighbors of other faiths, and acquire the skills for engagement that can help build communities of grace and generosity. I also wish that, as they read this text, congregations will also pray for discernment and the Holy Spirit's guidance on what being a follower of Jesus means for their witness to Christ as part of a loving response to their neighbors. As an Anabaptist I am convinced that in bold and courageous humility we must respect and welcome the neighbor, listen to their stories of faithfulness and obedience, love and appreciate them in their differentness, and, while resolutely disavowing coercion or manipulation, witness to the purposes of God that we see fulfilled in Jesus Christ.

Stanley W. Green
Executive Director
Mennonite Mission Network
May 2006

APPENDIX 1

INTERFAITH DIALOGUE AND MULTIFAITH ACTION: NOT JUST A SOCIAL GATHERING

Interfaith dialogue is a popular notion today, especially in western countries where religious demographics are reflecting increased immigration and the effects of globalization. Some countries, such as the United Kingdom, with its colonial background, have more experience than others with immigration of people of non-Christian religions. Second-, third-, and fourth-generation Hindus, Sikhs, and Muslims now live in London and other British cities.

Canada's influx of refugees and immigrants has primarily come in the past thirty years. Canadians generally want to get to know their new neighbors and are intrigued by the diversity of religious traditions. Yet many Canadians are uncomfortable asking questions about faith and culture in social gatherings for fear they will offend. Religion is still a topic to be avoided in "polite conversation." Interfaith dialogue and education can help faith communities befriend their neighbors and co-workers so that helpful discussions can take place.

Interfaith activity is "not just a social gathering," but is also vital to peacemaking and justice-building, according to authors

R. Scott Appleby and Rabbi Marc Gopin.[80] Most religions have an ambiguous history. While religious leaders at times have supported wars and tribal violence, they also possess the capacity to resolve conflicts through appropriate application of theology and Scripture while speaking and acting to promote peace and justice in the midst of tension. Appleby and Gopin affirm the work of religious groups in providing safe places for people to meet and build networks that transcend conflicts. Without networking and positive communication among religious groups, peace is difficult, especially if stereotypes and prejudices predominate.

In Israel/Palestine, Yehuda Stolov of Interfaith Encounter reported that organizations working for peace and justice facilitated conversations among Muslims, Jews, Druze, and Christians. Interfaith dialogue was not neutral, even though Interfaith Encounter asked group participants to get to know each other before discussing difficult political issues such as the occupation. Interfaith Encounter developed group discussion formats and guidelines to focus on dialogue, not political issues. After getting to know each other, discussions about political issues had a more nuanced, personal, and conciliatory texture. No longer were the topics about strangers or abstract situations, but were the concerns of respected participants in the group.[81]

Formal and informal interfaith organizations are forming in many places. As people enter the multifaith world, they find this dialogue more complex and demanding than they imagined. Though invigorating, this work requires discipline and constantly struggling for balance amid paradox. As perspectives are shared and stories are told, the complexity of religion, economics, history, politics, and culture is uncovered and addressed while the interfaith organizations promote understanding of each other's experiences and viewpoints.

Interfaith organizations may seem a natural phenomenon, but there is much to learn from the experiences of groups and facilitators. An interfaith organization benefits from the experiments of others, especially those in conflict situations. Effective gatherings are purposeful and well facilitated. I have been impressed by the reflection of facilitators, staff, and participants as I have interviewed them in my travels to England and Israel/Palestine.

This essay is the result of my leading the multifaith organization Interfaith Grand River (IGR) in Waterloo Region, Ontario, for three years and then being on a four-month study sabbatical in Elkhart, Indiana; London; and Jerusalem. Hopefully this essay will begin further discussion as the nature and viability of interfaith organizations are explored.

BRIEF HISTORY OF INTERFAITH GROUPS

Interfaith activity has been primarily a lay movement of those who want to know and understand people from other religions better. Interfaith groups do not study world religions but offer opportunities to meet members of other faiths.

Many people travel to learn about other cultures. Through computers and electronic media, information about other cultures is brought into our homes. Globalization and other factors have increased immigration and an influx of refugees to North America and Europe. Many in the West want to be hospitable to newcomers and sincerely desire a safe and comfortable community for everyone. There is often a keen interest in learning more about multifaith neighbors, but a hesitation to ask individually about religion, so groups for conversation have emerged.

Scholars and religious leaders have become more involved as globalization increases and as cities become more religiously diverse. Their participation has brought additional resources, such as books, lectures, group facilitation, and conferences.

Pope John Paul II also encouraged interfaith discussion. The

Vatican sponsored the 1986 interfaith gathering in Assisi to celebrate St. Francis' journey to meet Muslim leaders in Palestine and Egypt during the Crusades.

In 1893, the Parliament of World Religions met in Chicago as the first major conference of religions from around the world. In 1993, the Parliament gathered again in Chicago to celebrate its centennial and to emphasize that this world phenomenon then had many local interfaith associations. The Parliament gathered again in 1999, this time in Cape Town, South Africa, and then in 2004 in Barcelona. There are plans for the Parliament to gather every five years. As a result of this and other work, diverse groups have begun meeting in many cities.[82]

Interfaith groups are still primarily grassroots organizations with few resources. A 2003 survey of groups in the United Kingdom described how some organizations have been around for many years. These include the International Association of Religious Freedom, founded in 1900, the World Council of Faiths founded 1936, and the Council of Christians and Jews, launched in 1942. But of the 140 organizations in the survey, 43 percent were started since 2000, and 46 percent of those had a budget of less than 500 pounds per year (less than 1,000 U.S. dollars).[83] The movement has grown in the United Kingdom because, with the increase in Muslims, Sikhs, and Hindus living there, local authorities are now expected to consult with the religious community.

No census of interfaith groups has occurred in the United States or Canada. Diana Eck at Harvard University's Pluralism Center has documented the increase in temples, mosques, synagogues, and other religious institutions. Her book *A New Religious America* records the experiences of many local religious groups as they acculturate to the American environment and as they experience prejudice and hostility from their neighbors. Some local groups have joined the North American Interfaith Network.[84] As in Britain, many are small associations with budgets to match and little or no connection to national coalitions or organizations.

September 11, 2001, resulted in a flurry of interfaith activity. Many Christians wanted to understand and embrace Muslims as neighbors and to prevent stereotyping. Many North Americans are aware of the detention of Japanese during World War II and stories of harassment of Germans during World War I. In this environment, how does one work for peace in neighborhoods and cities? How can people better understand each other?

WHAT'S IN A NAME?

Selecting the name "Interfaith" for Interfaith Grand River (IGR) was a careful choice of words, but in the United Kingdom, *interfaith* and *multifaith* have different connotations. The terms distinguish the purpose and character of the groups. In Israel/Palestine, the terms *interreligious* and *coexistence* are sometimes used.

Interfaith organizations can be worldwide, national, provincial, regional, citywide, or within a neighborhood. When a new group forms, issues such as who attends meetings, the group's principal focus, the structure of meetings, the format for discussion, and safety concerns need to be addressed. Organizations may differ in name and character, depending on who is invited to the group or organization.

Some consideration should be given to the terms used in naming a group and describing its work. Here are a few guidelines.

Ecumenical refers to a group in which all are Christian but from different denominations. In Canada and the United States, there are councils of churches that allow Christians to work together. Discussions are generally amicable and work is cooperative. However, it is not just a social gathering. The theological or worship differences may be great but all are Christians seeking better understanding in a setting of equal status and voice.

Interfaith can define a group or organization that is engaged in dialogue and interaction potentially leading to a greater understanding of the faith of those participating in the discussion. Interfaith groups provide a place and time for meeting people from other religions, listening to personal experiences, understanding theology and practices, and participating in faith activities together.

Interfaith discussions are sometimes termed *bilateral* when there are two distinct groups or viewpoints involved, as in a Jewish-Christian dialogue or a Hindu-Muslim dialogue. The two "sides" often have a dynamic agenda between them, and other faiths are not involved. The discussion may revolve around theological issues or around community issues, such as civil rights, affordable housing, or discrimination.

There are also *trilateral* discussions, with three religions involved. The discussion among the Abrahamic faiths—Judaism, Christianity and Islam—is an example of this. There have been many such discussions since September 11, as people of faith work to increase tolerance.

Multifaith is a descriptive term for organizations that include all religions present in a particular environment. Examples include IGR, which welcomes representatives from any faith group in the Waterloo Region who wish to participate and continue to encourage input by leaders from all faith expressions. Interfaith Network in the United Kingdom incorporates representatives from the country's primary religious communities, including Buddhism, Christianity, Hinduism, Islam, Judaism, Sikhism, and others with significant populations there. Interfaith Network representatives are selected by their faith communities, and some of its functions are connected with government ventures. Smaller faith communities are not on the network board but participate in local organizations.

Interfaith groups are often homogeneous in the sense that many are composed of all academics, all religious leaders, all women, or all students. This commonality usually has an impact on the content and style of discussion. For example, women may meet in each other's homes. Academics may have a more formal discussion, including the presentation of papers. Students or young adults may choose weekend retreats. Several interfaith group facilitators report that mixing lay members and clergy often does not work because clergy are seen as experts, so lay members listen rather than becoming involved. A number of interfaith groups have brought in faith leaders for an opening discussion to clarify theology or scriptures. Groups then met without clergy or theologians present.

Groups usually begin by learning to know each other and hearing personal faith journeys. These stories illustrate the "lived experience" of people of faith. When several people are from the same religion, participants' life journeys show how faith is seen and experienced differently within the same faith. Sometimes individuals also describe how people from one religion have been oppressed or stereotyped.

Important process questions emerge from these discussions:

- Can all people listen to these stories and different perspectives?
- Is the setting a safe place to speak as well as to listen? Does everyone speak?
- What happens when discussion delves into topics that are new to some in the group?

Generally interfaith discussions usually have facilitators and specific guidelines to keep the discussion focused and all participants feeling safe to talk.

In Israel/Palestine, an interfaith women's group that met for a year chose to celebrate religious feasts in each other's homes. Muslim women celebrated a Succoth meal with Jews in West Jerusalem, where few Arabs live or travel. Then the Jewish women went to Arab East Jerusalem for a meal to end Eid. Both times, the guests experienced fear of going into an unknown neighborhood. In each other's homes, they felt welcomed and were delighted in the conversation and the foods.

A group of young-adult Messianic Jews and Palestinian Christians went to the desert for an ecumenical discussion to learn about each other's religion and culture. The desert was an unfamiliar environment for both. They shared good common experiences that helped them bond and enabled them to talk about differences and stereotypes. They had never understood the issues from the perspective of "the other" and were able to address the political and religious issues directly.

The formal interfaith dialogue of religious leaders often involves the presentation of papers and discussions in the contexts of history, theology, and scriptures. These discussions often result in the ability to share in worship, in celebration, in new theological understandings, or in theological research. Sometimes the formal interfaith dialogue is opened by symbolic actions.

In the United Kingdom, the term *multifaith* often refers to an organization of religious groups that focuses on working on a common project or solving community problems. Dialogue and greater understanding often occur but are not the group's main focus. In many communities, a multifaith group is brought together by a local government or other institution that is facing a particular issue. In the United Kingdom these groups are working on issues of housing, education, prisons, and social services. National protocols have been established indicating how and when local authorities should work with mandated multifaith councils.

Some invitations to participate in a multifaith committee may come from another faith group or a voluntary agency. The Church of England has consulted with local governments to begin mandated councils. It and other Christian denominations have established multifaith committees that address issues confronted by religions in specific localities. In the English cities of Bradford and Leeds, Methodists and Anglicans are working with Muslims and other people of faith to establish community services and to advocate with local governments.

The British experience has demonstrated the need for multi-faith groups because many individuals from specific religions are clustered in particular neighborhoods. Leaders meeting together often advise the government through multifaith councils and then provide mechanisms for interfaith dialogue. This networking is an important factor for social cohesion and for breaking down stereotypes and prejudices.

My interviews with leaders of interfaith and multifaith organizations in the United Kingdom have shown the need for governments to work very concretely with these religious groups to address the needs of people of all faiths. Currently in Canada, governments are just realizing that they need to pay more attention to an environment with many religions. In United Kingdom, there are now specific protocols to bring religious leaders together to address community issues. As numbers of peoples of different faiths settle in North America, Canada and United States will need to respond in a similar way.

At the opening of the Ontario Parliament in 2003, a religious service was based on Christian traditions like the Lord's Prayer and incorporated many of symbols of the faith. Why can't a ceremony like that reflect Ontario's multifaith context, especially since MPPs are not only Christian, but also Muslim, Sikh, Hindu, and Jewish. The provincial government could establish an ad hoc multifaith commission to examine the opening session and bring recommendations to the legislature before the next election.

The Ontario Multifaith Council was established to "ensure adequate and appropriate religious services and spiritual care for persons in institutions and community-based agencies and programs."[85] Through a series of regional councils, a provincial board and connections with chaplains and other leaders from provincial faith communities, the council advises government and advocates for the religious needs of Ontario residents who are in or are affected by government-run institutions. This includes correctional and health facilities. The council's work includes restorative justice projects and assisting homeless offenders being released from prison.

Ontario's Interfaith Social Assistance Reform Coalition (ISARC) was formed in 1986 by the provincial Social Assistance Reform Commission (SARC). Because faith communities provided many health and social services for economically marginalized people, SARC wanted a multifaith review of their study and recommendations. ISARC continued as a multifaith advocacy organization, working on issues of hunger, housing, children, refugees, homelessness, disability, and social assistance. Representatives from the different religions learned more about each other's faiths while undertaking advocacy for the economically marginalized. Other objectives included providing a forum to discuss issues associated with poverty and to learn about poverty and injustice in the province.

Organizations sometimes function at both the multifaith and the interfaith levels. Many multifaith organizations provide mechanisms and support for interfaith dialogue. As leaders work together on projects, they engage in interfaith discussion that increases understanding and respect. In Israel/Palestine, a significant number of multifaith groups have emerged to research and work on projects involving water, a resource vital to everyone, regardless of their religion. The cooperation has led to greater respect and understanding.

The Interreligious Coordinating Council in Israel, with seventy-one member organizations, is primarily multifaith but engages in various interfaith functions. Among them, it

   •serves as a resource center and information clearinghouse,

- •discusses issues of mutual concern,
- •promotes interreligious and intercultural program initiatives, and
- •facilitates communication with public officials and religious leaders.

The council often works at multifaith and interfaith activities simultaneously.[86]

THE ISRAELI/PALESTINIAN MODEL

Interreligious is a term often used by organizations in Israel/Palestine. The Interreligious Coordinating Council in Israel (ICCI) connects a variety of religious communities and institutions to promote understanding and discussion. Sarah Bernstein, a staff person at ICCI, reports that a steering committee is important in working with the many religious groups in Israel. ICCI brings participants together for interfaith discussion but finds that individuals need to work on customs, beliefs, and theological issues because the more contentious issues in Israel/Palestine are very difficult. Political discussions become very animated in Israel as prejudices and stereotypes emerge quickly. Learning about all participants as individuals of faith is important. Bernstein describes ICCI as a tool for improving the relationships among different groups.[87]

Coexistence is another term often used in the Israeli/Palestinian environment, where these very different communities lack regular interaction. Coexistence work involves working together to show that "others" are not faceless, but real humans. Rabbi Arik Asherman has been employing this philosophy in his group, Rabbis for Human Rights. The group has undertaken symbolic and concrete projects, such as planting olive trees in regions of great controversy and arranging forums for discussion and the venting of the concerns of Jewish and Arab victims of violence.[88]

∾

Interfaith and *multifaith* are the primary terms in today's discussions. The distinction made in the United Kingdom between the two is helpful, even though there is some overlap. It is also helpful to know whether a group exists primarily for dialogue and discussion or for action or advising.

PURPOSE OF AN INTERFAITH GROUP

One of the first tasks for an organization is to define its purpose. In some situations, the group may be facilitated by a larger group or coalition. Interfaith Encounter, for example, organizes groups for women, students, young adults, lay members, or clergy. Other groups in Israel/Palestine have an immediate specific focus, such as water resources, with religious toleration as a larger ideal.

When new coalitions and organizations form, a first step should be to agree on purposes, goals, and activities. An incident of some kind can bring the people together as a group, but soon the group needs to focus on a purpose and mission statement.

The Roman Catholic Church has identified four types of interfaith discussion or encounter:

- •Dialogue of life—living together in friendship
- •Dialogue of social action—working for peace and justice
- •Dialogue of intellect—seeking deeper understandings and truth through discussion, debate, and research
- •Dialogue of religious experience—sharing insights from prayer and meditation.[89]

When IGR was formed in 2001, the Kitchener-Waterloo Council of Churches set an initial agenda before contacting possible participants and the religious organizations in the region. The purpose was both interfaith and multifaith. After meeting twice, the group decided to select a name and a purpose. Participants affirmed a structure of one-hour discussion and an hour-long airing of community concerns. A sub-group eventually affirmed a mission statement. In 2004 and 2005, IGR reviewed its purpose and organizational structure, which it decided to maintain.

JUDEO-CHRISTIAN LEADERSHIP

Leadership of these kinds of groups has come mainly from the Judeo-Christian community. There are some obvious reasons for this:

- Many refugees and immigrants are busy earning an income for their families and do not have time to engage in an interfaith organization. For example, one retired Sikh man said he had not found time for interfaith activities until his retirement. Establishing his family and making sure his children were well-educated had been his first priorities.
- Though refugees or immigrants desire acceptance of their religion and culture, they are at the same time working hard to assimilate to their new surroundings. Learning the customs of the dominant culture often takes priority. Until recently, new Canadians usually gave up native spiritual practices that would make them stand out. For example, Muslim women would not cover their hair, Sikhs cut their hair, and Jewish men avoided wearing yarmulkes in public. Not doing so, even for religious reasons, had been a hindrance to employment. The growing interfaith movement and the growing numbers of immigrants has in some communities increased tolerance and given many people the strength to retain or return to their spiritual practices.
- There are leadership differences among the different religions. Judaism and Christianity have clergy, many of whom are employed full time by a congregation or denomination. They sometimes see interfaith discussion

and education as part of their responsibility. In other faiths, leadership might be more focused on worship practices. Laity may be expected to represent the religion in the community, not the clergy. Some religions do not have clergy at all. Some religious leaders do not speak English and cannot participate in discussions.

- Westerners often want to know about a neighbor's faith, but in other countries, interfaith discussion is not seen as important or necessary, particularly in countries that have many faiths. In India, for example, people often grow up with Muslims, Hindus, Jains, Sikhs, and Christians all in the same neighborhood and learn early about these religions, especially if family members are practicing another faith. Being cordial and friendly is important, but interfaith discussion may not even be an acceptable topic in social gatherings.
- Some groups are uncomfortable with interfaith discussions. For example, some conservative Christian denominations do not have the theological basis to participate in interfaith discussion. In Waterloo Region, they have been invited numerous times, but have chosen not to participate or have been instructed by their leaders not to participate.

GUIDELINES FOR INTERFAITH GROUPS

The following guidelines for an interfaith organization have emerged from reading, discussions with groups in United Kingdom and Israel/Palestine, reflection on IGR's short history, and a previous attempt to begin an interfaith organization in Waterloo Region.

There should be no proselytizing. This is a cardinal rule. Christians need to be especially alert to the negative effects of crusades, missions, and evangelism. Often missionaries from western countries brought with them the economics, politics, and culture of their homelands, sometimes to the detriment of the people to whom they were ministering. Though there may be benefits, such as healthcare and education, natives may feel their religion and culture is under assault by western Christians.

Some religions, Judaism for example, do not proselytize. They have some converts, primarily through marriage. Islam can be very assertive in evangelism, but strongly feels the sting of Christianity's Crusades and other activities among Muslims. Hinduism and Buddhism welcome others. Hindus especially will resist proselytizing, based on the destructive influences of imperialism linked with Christianity in India's history. Buddhists are attracting North Americans because of an interest in meditation, yoga, and other practices.

The purpose of interfaith discussion is to learn about others' faiths. Respect for their traditions, beliefs, history, and values is essential, even though one may disagree with doctrine, interpretation of history, or practice.

No one religion should be in a majority. For most of North America and Europe, this means that Christians should remain in the minority in an interfaith group, even though they might be the overwhelming majority in the populace. In Israel, Jews should not be the majority in a group.

It is often difficult to contain the majority religion to a minority status because many want to participate, and this interest is positive. But in interfaith dialogue, facilitators should attempt to gather equal numbers of participants from each religion. Everyone feels freer to speak when representation from each religion is equal.

More than one person should represent each religion. The principle for this and the previous guideline is that all should have a voice. As topics are discussed, persons from the same religion can confer with one another. Less assertive people will know they have the support of others. Different participants may be more informed on some issues than others. Solidarity allows each person to speak and to figure out how his or her faith and traditions might relate to the experiences of others.

Power is always an issue. In most European and North American societies, Christianity has been the majority religion, sometimes even the state religion. How do we graciously open the doors and invite others into discussions and activities? We are so much a part of the culture that the symbols, language, and events refer to our faith, but not to the faiths of others. Some Christians might feel in the minority because their denomination is smaller or their beliefs are counter to the primary culture. Yet Christians assume a certain authority in the culture, especially compared to other religions.

Interfaith activist Daniel Rossing, an Orthodox Jew, explains that Jews in Israel must be sensitive to their power in interfaith settings. He reminds his fellow believers to be sensitive to the plurality and historic presence of Christians in Israel, to be aware of issues that may offend, and to keep in mind the "maze of relationships with the Islamic world." His advice is appropriate in North America and Europe as well.[90]

Some may groan about the hard work of recognizing power differentials, but it is essential for open conversation. While others are trying to be assertive and speak out, Christians need to spend more time listening. Facilitators need to be alert to power dynamics so that all have a chance to speak and participate.

Representatives should be chosen in different ways. Representatives of the participating faiths must be allowed to select their own representatives. Guidelines for representatives might include the following:

- Participants should have a good reputation in their community.
- Participants should understand their faith, tradition, and organization so that issues and concerns can be explained

to others. This would also mean facility in the language used for discussion.

• Participants should take information or concerns back to their faith community for reaction and response, which should be reported at the interfaith table.

• Participant should have realistic expectations of how their faith community might respond.

Some religious groups would not send a person they might see as clergy to represent them in an interfaith group. For example, priests in some faiths primarily assist in worship or meditation and have few functions outside the church or temple. Yet in the same religion, a priest or priestess might decide to be more proactive on community issues. Lay leaders often know what is realistic to expect from their "spiritual leaders."

Expect convergence and divergence. All must agree to be respectful and work at understanding the others' positions. Understanding, however, does not always mean agreement or convergence. For example, I am a pacifist. Participants from other religious traditions in an interfaith group may also be pacifists, even as they base their conviction on different religious traditions. Others in the interfaith group may not be pacifist. Each participant agrees to listen respectfully and to work at understanding. The end result does not need to be a common belief or perspective on an issue. Though this may happen, it is not the goal of the group or the meeting.

As IGR talked about the new chapel for a local hospital, several Buddhists expressed the desire for a "quiet room" where a patient could die with family and spiritual caregivers present. This "quiet room" would have nurses attending only as requested by the patient, family, or spiritual caregivers. The family and others would be allowed to stay for six to twelve hours after the patient died. Unexpectedly, all IGR members agreed that this was more significant than a chapel. Where hospital chaplains expected divergence, convergence occurred.

CONCLUSION

Interfaith and multifaith organizations create a dynamic encounter in which individuals become involved in listening and then voicing their faith. Understanding and respect occurs in a complex set of relationships that builds community among participants and results in energizing peace and justice in the larger environment. Commitment to the interfaith group and our own faith is needed. It is not just a social gathering but requires hard work as cultures, religions, and experiences from around the world are shared.

APPENDIX 2
INTERFAITH GRAND RIVER: A BRIEF HISTORY

Interfaith Grand River, a dynamic interfaith organization in Waterloo Region, Ontario, is an active coalition of leaders from different faith communities. IGR has no staff. Ad hoc committees and monthly meetings provide occasions for people of different religious backgrounds to get to know each other and address community concerns.

CONTEXT AND FOUNDING

Since the 1970s, Waterloo Region has become home to refugees and immigrants of diverse racial and religious backgrounds. Earlier in the twentieth century, the region became home to many people from Central and Eastern Europe. Hungarians, Germans, Romanians, and Yugoslavians established thriving cultural centers and churches. The two universities in the region accepted students and professors from the British Commonwealth and many from South Asia. After graduation, many students settled in the region, while others went home as jobs opened for them. As nations in western Africa gained independence, immigrants came from those countries also. Chileans emigrated as a result of political upheaval in their country. In 1978, refugees from Vietnam, Laos, and Cambodia were accepted into Canada, often sponsored by churches. Many found the region a very positive environment and encouraged their relatives living in other parts of Canada to resettle in Waterloo Region. Central Americans traveled across the United States and settled in the region beginning in the mid-1980s. As political turmoil intensified, people from Somalia, Rwanda, Iraq, Iran, Kurdistan, former Yugoslavia, and recently Colombia moved to the area as refugees. People from South Asia, China, and other countries immigrated for better jobs, to attend universities and colleges, or to provide increased opportunities for their children.

These changes brought new cultures and changed the texture of the faith community in the region. Sikhs built Gurdwaras, Muslim established mosques, Buddhists constructed temples and meditation centers, and Orthodox Christians opened churches. Hindus even remodeled a warehouse as a temple and brought statues of the gods from India.

The desire and need to create an interfaith group grew out of relationships at House of Friendship. As chaplaincy director of House of Friendship, a Christian agency serving economically and socially marginalized people, my job includes assisting staff to understand different cultural and religious traditions. Those to whom we minister are becoming increasingly diverse. At our emergency food hamper, an initial concern was to provide halal meat for Muslims. I got to know a local imam and began working with Sunni and Shi'a Muslim communities. We needed Muslims not only to donate halal meat but also to help sort other food products because the House of Friendship staff was unaware which food additives were unacceptable.

There had been an earlier attempt to form an interfaith association, but the group that formed did not take time to get to know each other and develop a purpose statement. Some participants were interested in developing interfaith programs for youth and adults. The leadership was primarily two Christian pastors and a Jewish rabbi. Very few non-Christians joined the group. Several issues made it difficult for this interfaith group to emerge:

- The majority of participants were Christian.
- The focus too quickly became "programs" for youth.
- Sikh, Buddhist, Hindu, Muslim, and other non-Christians newcomers had not established communities or even built structures for worship.
- The group did not take time to invite and network with people of other faiths.
- The group did not have a sponsoring organization.

This group of Christian, Jewish, Quaker, and Buddhist leaders met for half a year and then fizzled out.

INTERFAITH GRAND RIVER BEGINS

After I joined the Kitchener Waterloo Council of Churches in 2000 as its Mennonite representative, the council's executive discussed forming an interfaith group. Three executive members from local council took the spring and summer of 2001 to identify and contact leaders of the different faith communities in Waterloo Region. These leaders agreed to a first meeting on Thursday, September 13, 2001. The council agreed that I would facilitate the first meeting and another council member would take the minutes.

Two days after the terrorist attacks on September 11, the new interfaith group met and agreed that our gathering was important, especially in times of such community tension. Leaders from different faith communities needed to get to know each other personally and become acquainted with other religions so that we could work together to overcome tension and resolve conflicts. The group agreed to have one hour for discussing a topic and learning different faith traditions' practices, traditions, and theology. The second hour would focus on activities and issues in the region as well as the business of the organization.

The first meeting included Reform Jews, Sikhs, Sunni Muslims, Unitarians, and Christians from denominations including Anglican, Catholic, Lutheran, Mennonite, Presbyterian, and United Church of Canada. Leaders from the Unity Centre for Practical Christianity also participated. One hospital chaplain was present. It was agreed to contact leaders of other religions, including the Buddhist, Hindu, neopagan, Quaker, and Shi'a Muslim faiths. Christian Science, Orthodox Judaism, and Scientology leaders joined the coalition in the following years. Aboriginal, evangelical Christian, and Orthodox Christian leaders were invited but did not attend. A Coptic Orthodox priest asked for minutes and plans to attend as invited or able.

At typical meetings, the first hour of discussion is often lively, interesting, and helpful. No topic is ever thoroughly discussed, often leaving participants wanting to learn more and to explore their own tradition further as a result of the interaction.

Discussion topics have included

- What is the meaning of life?
- What does *faith* mean in your tradition?
- What is the meaning and place of ritual?
- What do we mean by ethics?
- How does religion relate to government?
- How is death viewed? What happens at the time of death?

One local hospital was building a large cancer center and moving the chapel. The chaplains consulted the interfaith group about spiritual needs and about the design of the chapel.

The chaplains were surprised that all religions wanted to have a private room where spiritual caregivers, family members, and others could quietly be present with the dying person. Though some nursing and medical support could be needed, the preference was for minimal contact unless requested. Buddhists asked that they be allowed to stay with a body for six to twelve hours after death and that there be a window so the spirit of the person could escape. Other religions wished to remain in the room so members could wash the body before burial or cremation within the same day. These concerns were reported to the hospital administration.

The new chapel was named Sanctuary, a word that in all religions meant a quiet and safe space. All faith communities appreciated the simplicity of the room with symbols and scriptures stored in cupboards, so they could be used when needed by a particular religion. Otherwise the room was a quiet place with both chairs and floor pillows. The one request of all traditions was that there be water near the entrance for ritual washing and other uses. Unfortunately the chapel was already designed for an area without easy access to plumbing and water. It was a very plain room with scriptures and ritual objects available in cupboards. Chairs and kneeling cushions were available.

The group requested a local religion and media professor to help it focus its concerns about relating to newspapers, radio, and television. These included:

- How can faith communities contact media to publicize local events and special celebrations?
- How can faith communities help reporters understand and interpret religious events and perspectives?
- How do faith communities help adherents, especially youth, understand the effects of advertising? Can faith communities effectively counter the materialism and sec-

ular ethics portrayed in television shows and news programs? How can family and religion have more influence
than the media?

Starting in 2002, IGR met with reporters and editors of the
local newspaper and the television station. The newspaper had
hired a religion reporter who consulted with members for news
stories, features on local religions, and pictures of the different
celebrations and activities in the region. He consulted with religious leaders when there was a faith perspective in local,
national, or world events. He did a primarily pictorial series
called "The Way We Pray" in the center fold of the Perspectives
section of the weekend paper, which was well received by readers of all faiths. His collaborative work did much to help area
residents appreciate the growing multifaith texture of the community.

The local television station also met with the group, but
there were no significant contacts or follow-up after the initial
meeting.

Beginning in November 2001, the group worked hard on
developing a statement of purpose and choosing a name.
"Interfaith" was easy, but how to name the geographic area
was more difficult. The Grand River is a major waterway in
the region, and many congregations dot the cities and towns
adjacent to it. For this reason, and because rivers and water are
often used as religious imagery, "Grand River" was chosen as
the second part of the name.

The purpose statement took five months to craft. A recently edited version is in appendix 3.

A two-day seminar for teachers, principals, and social
workers called Safer Schools: Safer Communities asked IGR to
present a panel on religious toleration and to provide morning
devotions each day of the conference. Volunteers from the
group handled both requests.

As the first summer of its existence approached, IGR focused on how and whether to mark the first anniversary of September 11. Buddhist leaders suggested holding a "peace walk" with all participants keeping silence for the entire march. Others suggested that each tradition present a prayer, chant, or song about justice and peace at the end of the walk. Would local politicians approve this walk? Were they planning a memorial service themselves?

Local mayors and the regional chairperson were concerned that a memorial service or peace walk would increase ethnic and religious tensions in the area. They preferred to do nothing. Because of the war in Afghanistan, some IGR members wanted to disassociate themselves with this action of the United States government. But other IGR members felt that the anniversary should be noted in some way out of respect for all who had died, including many firemen, police, and emergency service workers.

The peace walk went from the center of Waterloo to a park in downtown Kitchener. There participants stood quietly while people from ten different traditions offered prayers for peace and justice in the world. The silence was then broken, and participants had good conversations. Police, firefighters, and emergency workers thanked the IGR organizers, saying they hoped their colleagues lost in New York would again be remembered a year later.

IGR decided to continue the annual peace walk but not to hold it on the September 11. The itinerary varied. Sometimes a vegetarian potluck was held at a local church. A prayer service concluded each walk.

Discussions at IGR in the following years included responses to the war in Iraq, secularism, good and evil, the Earth Charter of the United Nations, secular ethics, older persons and spiritual care, mental health, and spirituality in the school systems. Another topic was spiritual care for those with HIV/AIDS.

IGR and local hospital chaplains worked together with AIDS organizations to provide a list of spiritual-care givers from all religious traditions. The list is updated regularly and several volunteers from IGR have worked with AIDS organizations and the Waterloo Region Public Health to provide training for lay and clergy spiritual-care givers.

The coordinator of the Governor General's Canadian Leadership Conference approached IGR to provide a seminar on religious diversity and to host the young adults participating in it. Old Order Mennonites hosted them the first day, followed by the diverse IGR participants on the second day. Morning discussion was lively. Many young adult leaders appreciated seeing Canada's diverse religions talking together in one region.

IGR's purpose was tested after some gravestones were destroyed at a local Jewish cemetery. Could the community come together to support the Jewish community? A solidarity evening at the synagogue, planned by the synagogue's executive committee, invited only Jewish speakers. The standing-room-only crowd of seven hundred included Sikhs, Muslims, Hindus, Unitarians, Christians of all traditions, and many others. Some attending were Palestinian and Egyptian. Several speakers, including a Holocaust survivor, were very inspiring.

Toward the close of the gathering, the president of the synagogue asked that all stand to sing the Israeli national anthem. All stood politely as the anthem was sung, but there was much discussion about it as people left the service. At the next IGR meeting, the rabbi apologized for the singing of the anthem. He said he had requested that other leaders speak, but the synagogue executive decided the evening's program. The apology was accepted by IGR.

Kitchener Waterloo Council of Churches held a series of six supper meetings over two years. Each featured a speaker from one of the major faiths worshipping in the area. Christian leaders moderated the meeting, and some dialogue took place. IGR provided the panels for these meetings.

IGR was encouraged by community residents who could not participate in weekday morning IGR meetings to hold interfaith activities and educational opportunities so others could learn about the faiths of new immigrants. IGR made arrangements with Encounter: World Religions to conduct a fall and spring series of seminars on the different religions worshipping in the area. Each series had thirteen sessions, starting with an introduction to religions of the area. Each week after that, an educational session explained one religion. During the following weekend, participants were invited to attend a service in that religious tradition. Six religions were part of the fall session; six additional religions were in the spring session. And the seminar series continues.

In fall of 2004, a television talk show held a panel discussing terrorism. Participants on the panel included the provocative show host, a Jewish representative, a local Muslim leader, a Muslim lawyer, and an expert on terrorism. The Jewish representative and Muslim leader made some very confrontational statements about Jews and Palestinians, which were picked up by national and international media. At the request of the organization, the Jewish representative resigned his position with B'nai B'rith. The Muslim leader was questioned by his employer and by the regional police.

Tension escalated in the community, and even IGR found the situation difficult to discuss. Would working at conflict resolution on this issue break up the group? Was IGR viable if it did not address issues of conflict like this? Some on the steering committee were very discouraged when a Hindu brought forward the tensions between Hindus and Muslims in India. After some discussion, it was agreed that IGR would watch the videotape of the television show and discuss it at a monthly meeting.

For that meeting, very few were absent. The consensus after the viewing was that some media had misrepresented the statements of the panel members. IGR agreed that six members representing different religions, including a Jew and Muslim, would meet with the Muslim leader from the television talk show in a truth and healing circle. Since the Jewish leader was from Toronto, he was not involved in IGR's conflict mediation process. Truth and healing circles are a Canadian aboriginal method of dealing with community tension. Participants in a conflict sit in a circle or at a table and one-by-one talk about their understanding of the conflict and their relationships with others at the table. They attempt to place the issues, emotions and concerns in the circle and then search for a way of settling the conflict. This was very helpful for the Muslim leader and for IGR. The results were reported and accepted at the next meeting.

IGR recently has been researching how schools can provide training in concentration, meditation, and compassion for teachers and students. IGR members are concerned that children and youth become open to various spiritual ideas and forms of meditation. How are the spiritual needs of students addressed in a multifaith region? After much research and discussion with school officials, a committee from IGR held an all-day retreat using various methods of concentration and meditation. The words *spirituality* and *religion* are never used. IGR is investigating other areas where meditation and concentration techniques are used and researched for results. Conversation continues with the school board.

As IGR continues, it is frequently consulted by organizations and regional governments. It has become a forum for learning about people from other traditions and a place where some religious tensions can be resolved or at least discussed. Providing understanding of the role of religions and shedding light on their diversity continues to be an important purpose.

QUESTIONS FOR DISCUSSION AND REFLECTION

1. Would you participate in an interfaith forum? How would you listen to and respect diverse theological positions from different religions?
2. Would you be able to represent your denomination and tradition to others who are not Christian? What aspects of your religion's history, theology, and sociology guide your presence in this discussion?
3. Interfaith discussion includes convergence and divergence in theology, faith practices, lifestyles, worship, and prayer. Would you be able to agree and disagree with others while keeping respectful their beliefs and attitudes?
4. Of the issues faced by IGR, what intrigued you the most? Did you desire to be present for the discussion or to research the issues further? What issues would have been most difficult for you if you had been sitting around the table at these discussions? Why?

APPENDIX 3

STATEMENT OF PURPOSE: INTERFAITH GRAND RIVER

We come together here with the following understanding of our common purpose:

We are persons of different faith communities, spiritual traditions, cultures, races, colors, and genders. Our differences are religious, linguistic, geographical, cultural, and personal. It is precisely our differences that bring us together.

From diverse backgrounds, we strive to live harmoniously as one community. We cultivate an environment of tolerance, understanding, respect, trust, mutual support, and ultimately love. We seek to develop and celebrate an awareness of our interdependence.

On the basis of these principles, Interfaith Grand River brings the wisdom of our many traditions to bear on current issues affecting our community.

Our objectives are:
1. To promote dialogue among our different traditions, leading to understanding and respect
2. To provide a forum for the discussion of contemporary issues in the context of diverse religious perspectives
3. To challenge expression of religious and other intolerance in the community.

4. To provide support for and to encourage networking among people working in a variety for religious contexts
5. To provide shared spiritual experiences for people representing a variety of religious practices
6. To deepen knowledge of the commonalities and differences among religious and spiritual traditions
7. To acknowledge and celebrate the religious and spiritual diversity of our community
8. To learn from and be enriched by the interaction among our respective spiritual and religious traditions.

May 2005

APPENDIX 4

RELIGIOUS CEREMONIES INVOLVING MORE THAN ONE FAITH: GUIDELINES FROM THE CANADIAN COUNCIL OF CHURCHES

INTRODUCTION

At certain times in Canadian public life, significant events call on the resources of the religious and spiritual traditions of our land. These might be occasions of public mourning, as in the case of the crash of the Swissair Flight 111 near Peggy's Cove. They might be solemn events, such as the bringing home of the Unknown Soldier to Ottawa in the summer of 2000. They could be moments celebrating our history, such as the memorializing of the "Famous Five Women" from the Persons Case. In communities across our land, Thanksgiving Day is often marked with multifaith celebrations.

The Canadian Council of Churches (CCC) offers the following guidelines as a contribution toward acknowledging the multifaith realities of our country. Developed by the CCC Interfaith Relations Committee in consultation with partners from the Muslim and Jewish families, and adopted as a statement of the Council, these guidelines provide suggestions for planning and conducting public religious ceremonies that include the participation of a diversity of religious traditions.

GUIDELINES

Prayer involving members of more than one religious tradition is appropriate on public occasions when the wider community comes together to celebrate, or to mourn following a tragedy. As members of diverse communities in consultation with one another we have made the following recommendations to our constituencies.

Such religious ceremonies grow out of, and reflect, respect for all traditions present. This respect needs to be present in the planning as well as in the actual event. Faith communities should take the initiative to work collaboratively in planning such events. They are free to name their own leadership to participate in planning and in the actual prayer.

- Introductory bidding prayers should be inclusive, in the form of an invocation that opens the community to the divine presence. Sensitivity toward all participants ought to guide all activities.
- Each participating leader should be free to pray from within his or her own tradition, and to read from texts that are considered sacred in his or her own tradition.
- Leaders may speak positively about their own tradition, not negatively about other faith traditions.
- It is appropriate to pray individually and collectively for the good and well-being of the whole community gathered. It is inappropriate in this context to offer prayers which imply incompleteness of another faith tradition.

The aim of such religious ceremonies is to foster that respectful presence which enables members of a community to support and affirm each other. These guidelines give all participants the freedom to speak from their own traditions faithfully, and the responsibility to respect other traditions fully.[91]

NOTES

INTRODUCTION

1. Information from friend in the Chicago United Methodist bishop's office.

2. An example is *Faith in My Neighbor: World Religions in Canada* (Toronto: United Church of Canada, 1994), which gives a brief introduction to each of the major world religions in Canada. In *A New Religious American* (San Francisco: HarperCollins, 2001), Diana Eck portrays the history and struggle of non-Christian religions in United States. Robert Choquette offers a history of religion, including Christianity, in *Canada's Religions* (Ottawa: University of Ottawa Press, 2004).

CHAPTER 1: SPIRITUALITY AND TRANSFORMATION

3. Carolyn Gratton, *The Art of Spiritual Guidance* (New York: Crossroad, 1992), 5.

4. "The Earth Charter" can be found on the web at www.earthcharter.org.

5. James Fowler, *Stages of Faith and Religious Development* (New York: Crossroad, 1991).

6. Halal is very similar to kosher in Judaism. *Halal* means meat has come from an animal that has a particular type of hoof, that has been killed in a certain way, and that has been butchered in a place inspected and prayed over by imams.

7. Khalsa is a Sikh spiritual and military order, established in 1699. Practices, such as wearing the turban and not cutting hair are spiritual disciplines keeping the person constantly aware of God.

8. Rosemary Houghton, "Conflict and Resolution: The Transformation of Man," in *Conversion*, Walter E. Conn, ed. (New York: Alba House, 1978), 23.

9. William H. Willimon, *Acts: Interpretation Bible Commentary* (Atlanta: John Knox Press, 1988), 95-105.

10. Chalmer W. Faw, *Acts: Believers Church Bible Commentary* (Scottdale, Pa.: Herald Press, 1993), 124-30.

11. *Stake* is a term for the congregational unit in the Church of Jesus Christ of the Latter Day Saints.

CHAPTER 2: HOSPITABLE AND INCLUSIVE

12. Christine Pohl, *Making Room: Recovering Hospitality as a Christian Tradition* (Grand Rapids, Mich.: Wm. B. Eerdmans Publishing, 1999), 4.

13. Robert J. Suderman, "Reflections on hospitality and the missional church," *Vision*, Spring 2002, 46-7.

14. Eleanor Epp Stobbe, *Practicing God's Hospitality* (doctoral thesis, Emmanuel College, Toronto School of Theology, April 2000), 145-48.

15. Jean Vanier, *Becoming Human* (Toronto: House of Anansi Press, 1998), 69-103.

16. Marcus Borg, *The Heart of Christianity* (San Francisco: HarperCollins, 2003), 151-54.

17. Miroslav Volf, *Exclusion and Embrace* (Nashville: Abingdon Press, 1996), 52.

18. To attach is to lose freedom because habits, behaviors, ideals, or the need to control are connected to our ability to relate to another person. To detach means we are free and open to receiving the other person as he or she is, without stereotyping or making prejudicial judgments.

19. Gerald May, *Addiction and Grace* (San Francisco: HarperCollins, 1988), 1-17.

20. King Herod at Jesus birth was not the same person as King Herod as at Jesus' crucifixion.

21. Borg, 155-56.

22. May, 4-11

23. *The Interpreter's Bible*, vol. 2 (Nashville: Abingdon Cokesbury Press, 1953), 852.

CHAPTER 3: MOVING TOWARD DIALOGUE

24. Concepts on this journey are identified by David Lochhead in *The Dialogical Imperative: A Christian Reflection on Interfaith Encounter* (Maryknoll, N.Y.: Orbis, 1988).

25. Ibid., 8-9.

26. I have used the Mennonite community as an example because I know the history, experiences, and many nuances of my Mennonite tradition.

27. http://en.wikipedia.org/wiki/immigration_to_Israel_from_Arab_lands#Iraq

28. Bishop C. Joseph Sprague, then United Methodist Bishop of Chicago, reported this in a personal conversation in 2003.

29. Includes Serbian, Greek, Romanian, Ukrainian, and other Orthodox, which was double the population in 1991. Many have come as refugees from former Yugoslavia as well as other Eastern European countries.

30. *Kitchener-Waterloo Record*, September 30, 2003, A1-2.

31. www.religioustolerance.org/can_rel2.htm

32. www.adherents.com/rel_USA.htm

33. *Kitchener-Waterloo Record*, October 1, 2003, A1-2.

34. Margaret Macmillan, *Paris 1919: Six Months that Changed the World* (New York: Random House, 2003).

35. Henri Nouwen, *Reaching Out: Three Movements of the Spiritual Life* (Garden City, N.Y.: Doubleday, 1975), 47.

36. R. Scott Appleby, *The Ambivalence of the Sacred* (Latham, Md.: Rowman and Littlefield Publishers, 2000), 12-13.

37. www.adherents.com/rel_USA.htm

38. Joseph Liechty and Cecelia Clegg, *Moving Beyond Sectarianism: Religion, Conflict, and Responsibility in Northern Ireland* (Dublin: Columba Press, 2001).

39. Appleby, 16.

40. Nouwen, 53.

41. Lochhead, 18.

42. Nouwen, 50-1.

43. Lochhead, 38.

A MULTIFAITH EXPERIENCE: REMEMBER ABRAHAM . . .

44. I use the spelling of Ishmael from the NRSV Bible because I am writing for a Christian audience. Muslim texts might use spellings such as Ismel, Ismail, or Isma'il.

45. Walter Brueggemann, *Genesis: Interpretation: A Bible Commentary for Teaching and Preaching* (Atlanta: John Knox Press, 1982), 152.

46. Ibid., 235.

47. Marc Gopin, *Holy War, Holy Peace* (New York: Oxford University Press, 2002), 10.

48. Ibid.

49. Brueggemann, 153.

50. Eugene Roop, *Genesis: Believers Church Bible Commentary* (Scottdale, Pa.: Herald Press, 1987), 119.

51. Ibid., 139.

52. Brueggemann, 151.

CHAPTER 4: STRUGGLING TO BECOME NORTH AMERICAN

53. Robert Choquette, *Canada's Religions* (Ottawa: University of Ottawa Press, 2004), 379.

54. *Kitchener-Waterloo Record*, June 18, 2005, A10.

55. These statistics were compiled by the author from Canadian census data and unpublished projections completed by the planning department of the Region of Waterloo.

56. *Kitchener-Waterloo Record*, September 30, 2003, A1.

57. Cynthia Keppley Mahmood, "Sikhs in Canada: Identity and Commitment" in *Religion and Ethnicity in Canada* (Toronto: Pearson Longman, 2005), 52-3.

58. Mahmood, 59.

59. For an account of one Hmong family's difficulties, especially as they struggled to keep their traditions and religious practices, see Anne Fadiman's *The Spirit Catches You and You Fall Down* (New York: Farrar, Straus and Giroux, 1997). They encounter unfamiliar medical practices in contrast to the rituals and herbs they've traditionally used for their daughter's seizures.

60. Cynthia Keppley Mahmood, "Sikhs in Canada: Identity and Commitment" in *Religion and Ethnicity in Canada*, op. cit., 53.

61. Ibid., 54.

A MULTIFAITH EXPERIENCE: CEDAR'S QUESTION

62. This history is told by Ilan Pappe, *A History of Modern Palestine* (Cambridge: Cambridge University Press, 2004), 131-41. Pappe is a Jewish professor at the University of Haifa. His book is controversial because he attempts to be objective about both Palestinian and Jewish actions, rather than writing from one side.

63. From Sabeel's Purpose statement. Available at www.sabeel.org.

64. This quote from Cedar is recounted from the author's notes of her presentation at Tantur.

65. Their books are listed in the bibliography.

CHAPTER 5: SEEING OUR WORLD DIFFERENTLY

66. Reginald Bibby, *Restless Gods* (Toronto: Stoddart Publishing, 2002), 83-4.

CHAPTER 6: CAN WE BECOME A MULTIFAITH SOCIETY?

67. Douglas John Hall, *The End of Christendom and the Future of Christianity* (Valley Forge, Pa.: Trinity Press, 1997), vii–ix.

68. Ibid., 20-21.

69. Ibid., 41ff.

70. R. Scott Appleby, *The Ambivalence of the Sacred* (Lanham, Md.: Rowman and Littlefield Publishers, 2000), 8-27.

CHAPTER 7: BEGINNING WITH LOVE

71. Pheme Perkins, *First and Second Peter, James and Jude (Interpretation: A Bible Commentary for Teaching and Preaching)* (Louisville, Ky.: John Knox Press, 1995), 84-114.

72. John Miller, *Step by Step Through the Parables* (New York: Paulist Press, 1981), 79.

73. Jean Vanier, *Becoming Human* (New York: Paulist Press, 1998), 78-9.

74. Marcus Borg, *The Heart of Christianity* (San Francisco: HarperCollins, 2003), 122-3.

75. Harriet Crabtree, *Local Interfaith Activity in the U.K.: A Survey* (London: The Interfaith Network, 2003), vii.

76. Available on the Internet from Methodist Church House at www.methodist.org.uk under Information and Inter Faith.

AFTERWORD

77. Hans Kung, "Ecumenism and Truth: The Wider Dialogue," *The Tablet*, vol. 233 (1989).

78. Lesslie Newbigin, *The Finality of Christ* (Richmond, Va.: John Knox, 1969).

79. Ibid.

APPENDIX 1: INTERFAITH DIALOGUE AND MULTIFAITH ACTION

80. R. Scott Appleby, *The Ambivalence of the Sacred* (Lanham, Md.: Rowman and Littlefield, 2000), and Marc Gopin, *Holy War, Holy Peace* (Oxford: Oxford University Press, 2002).

81. Personal discussion on December 16, 2004.

82. Diana Eck, *A New Religious America* (San Francisco: HarperCollins, 2001), 371-2.

83. *Local Interfaith Activity in the UK: A Survey* (London: The InterFaith Network, 2003), vii.

84. Eck, 372.

85. From the Ontario Multifaith Council's website www.omc.ca.

86. *Guide to Interreligious and Intercultural Activities in Israel*, the 2001 ICCR guide and annual report, v, vi. The report is not listed in ICCI's publications, but information is available through their web site at www.icci.co.il. See the Members page and the Internet Links page.

87. Conversation with Sarah Bernstein on December 6, 2004.

88. Interview with Rabbi Arik Asherman on December 10, 2004.

89. *Faith Meeting Faith* (London: The Methodist Church, 2004), 57.

90. Daniel Rossing, "Preparing for Dialogue in the Holy Land," *America*, September 13, 2004, 18-21.

APPENDIX 4: RELIGIOUS CEREMONIES GUIDELINES

91. From Canadian Council of Churches web site: www.ccc-cce.ca.

BIBLIOGRAPHY

Abhishiktananda. *The Secret of Arunachala*. Delhi: I.S.P.C.K., 1979.

———. *Hindu Christian Meeting Point*. Delhi: I.S.P.C.K., 1969.

Antoun, Richard T. *Understanding Fundamentalism: Christian, Islamic, and Jewish Movements*. New York: Altamira Press, 2001.

Appleby, R. Scott. *The Ambivalence of the Sacred: Religion, Violence, and Reconciliation*. Lanham, Md.: Rowman and Littlefield Publishers, 2000.

Arai, Tosh, and Wesley Ariarajah. *Spirituality in Interfaith Dialogue*. Geneva: WCC Publications, 1989.

Ariarajah, S. Wesley. *Not Without My Neighbor: Issues in Interfaith Relations*. Geneva: WCC Publications, 1999.

Bibby, Reginald W. *Restless Gods: The Renaissance of Religion in Canada*. Toronto: Stoddart Publishing, 2002.

Bishop, Morris. *Saint Francis of Assisi*. Boston: Little, Brown and Company, 1974.

Borg, Marcus J. *The Heart of Christianity*. San Francisco: HarperCollins, 2003.

Bramadat, Paul, and David Seljak, eds. *Religion and Ethnicity in Canada*. Toronto: Pearson Education Canada, 2005.

Brueggemann, Walter, and George Stroup. *Many Voices, One God: Being Faithful in a Pluralistic World*. Louisville, Ky.: Westminster/John Knox, 1998.

Bryant, M. Darrol. *Religion in a New Key: Three Lectures.* Kitchener, Ontario: Pandora Press, 2001.

Burrell, David B. *Friendship and Ways to Truth.* Notre Dame, Ind.: University of Notre Dame Press, 2000.

Carter, Stephen L. *The Culture of Disbelief: How American Law and Politics Trivialize Religious Devotion.* New York: Basic Books, 1993.

Choquette, Robert. *Canada's Religions: An Historical Introduction.* Ottawa: University of Ottawa Press, 2004.

Cobb, John, ed. *Christian Faith and Religious Diversity: Mobilization for the Human Family.* Minneapolis: Fortress Press, 2002.

Conn, Walter. *Christian Conversion: A Developmental Interpretation of Autonomy and Surrender.* New York: Paulist Press, 1986.

Coward, Harold. *Pluralism: Challenge to World Religions.* Maryknoll, N.Y.: Orbis, 1984.

Dupuis, Jacques. *Christianity and the Religions: From Confrontation to Dialogue.* Maryknoll, N.Y.: Orbis, 2002.

Eck, Diana L. *A New Religious America: How a "Christian Country" has Become the World's Most Religiously Diverse Nation.* San Francisco: HarperCollins, 2001.

Ellis, Marc H. *Toward a Jewish Theology of Liberation: The Challenge of the 21st Century.* Maryknoll, N.Y.: Orbis, 1989.

Fadiman, Anne. *The Spirit Catches You and You Fall Down.* New York: Farrar, Straus and Giroux, 1997.

Gopin, Marc. *Holy War, Holy Peace: How Religion Can Bring Peace to the Middle East.* New York: Oxford University Press, 2002.

Hall, Douglas John. *The End of Christendom and The Future of Christianity.* Valley Forge, Pa.: Trinity Press, 1997.

Hick, John. *The Fifth Dimension: An Exploration of the Spiritual Realm.* Oxford: One World, 1999.

Ingham, Michael. *Mansions of the Spirit: The Gospel in a Multifaith World*. Toronto: Anglican Book Centre, 1997.

Kateregga, Badru D., and David W. Shenk. *A Muslim and A Christian in Dialogue*. Scottdale, Pa.: Herald Press, 1997.

Kimball, Charles. *Striving Together: A Way Forward in Christian-Muslim Relations*. Maryknoll, N.Y.: Orbis, 1991.

Knitter, Paul F. *One Earth Many Religions: Multifaith Dialogue and Global Responsibility*. Maryknoll, N.Y.: Orbis, 1995.

Kung, Hans, and Karl-Josef Kuschel, eds. *A Global Ethic: The Declaration of the Parliament of World Religions*. New York: Continuum, 1995.

Liechty, Joseph, and Cecelia Clegg. *Moving Beyond Sectarianism: Religion, Conflict, and Reconciliation*. Dublin: Columba Press, 2001.

Lochhead, David. *The Dialogical Imperative: A Christian Reflection on Interfaith Encounter*. Maryknoll, N.Y.: Orbis, 1988.

McAvity, Marks. *Faith in My Neighbor: World Religions in Canada*. Toronto: United Church of Canada, 1994.

Methodist Church. *The Life We Share*. London: Methodist Church, 2003.

Munayer, Salim J., ed. *In the Footsteps of Our Father Abraham*. Bethlehem, West Bank: Masalaha, 1993.

————. *Seeking and Pursuing Peace*. Bethlehem: Masalaha, 1998.

Mwakabana, Hance C. *Multifaith Challenges Facing the Americas . . . and Beyond*. Geneva: Lutheran World Federation, 2002.

Newbigin, Lesslie. *The Gospel in a Pluralist Society*. Grand Rapids, Mich.: Wm. B. Eerdmans, 1989.

Panikkar, Raymond. *The Trinity and World Religions*. Madras, India: Christian Literature Society, 1970.

Perkins, Pheme. *First and Second Peter, James and Jude (Interpretation: A Bible Commentary for Teaching and Preaching)*. Louisville, Ky.: John Knox Press, 1995.

Pieris, Aloysius. *Love Meets Wisdom: A Christian Experience of Buddhism*. Maryknoll, N.Y.: Orbis, 1988.

Pohl, Christine D. *Making Room: Recovering Hospitality as a Christian Tradition*. Grand Rapids, Mich.: Wm. B. Eerdmans, 1999.

Raheb, Mitri, trans. by Ruth C. L. Gritsch. *I Am a Palestinian Christian*. Minneapolis: Fortress Press, 1995.

Ramadan, Tariq. *Western Muslims and the Future of Islam*. Oxford; New York: Oxford University Press, 2004.

Schlabach, Gerald. *And Who Is My Neighbor? Poverty, Privilege, and the Gospel of Christ*. Scottdale, Pa.: Herald Press, 1990.

Shenk, Calvin. *Who Do You Say That I Am? Christians Encounter Other Religions*. Scottdale, Pa.: Herald Press, 1997.

Smith, Huston. *Why Religion Matters: The Fate of the Human Spirit in an Age of Disbelief*. San Francisco: HarperCollins, 2001.

Smith, William Cantwell. *Faith and Belief*. Princeton: Princeton University Press, 1979.

Suchocki, Marjorie Hewitt. *Divinity and Diversity: A Christian Affirmation of Religious Pluralism*. Nashville: Abingdon Press, 2003.

Swimme, Brian. *The Hidden Heart of the Cosmos: Humanity and the New Story*. Maryknoll, N.Y.: Orbis, 1996.

Thomas, M. *Risking Christ for Christ's Sake*. Geneva: WCC Publications: 1987.

Tschuy, Theo. *Ethnic Conflict and Religion: Challenge to the Churches*. Geneva: WCC Publications, 1997.

Vanier, Jean. *Becoming Human*. Toronto: House of Anansi Press, 1998.

Volf, Miroslav. *Exclusion and Embrace: A Theological Exploration of Identity, Otherness, and Reconciliation.* Nashville: Abingdon Press, 1996.

Wiles, Maurice. *Christian Theology and Inter-religious Dialogue.* Philadelphia: Trinity Press, 1992.

Yong, Amos. *Beyond the Impasse: Toward a Pneumatological Theology of Religions.* Grand Rapids, Mich.: Baker Academic, 2003.

Young, Pamela Dickey. *Christ in a Post-Christian World.* Minneapolis: Fortress Press, 1995.

THE AUTHOR

Brice H. Balmer is chaplain at House of Friendship, a Christian, non-profit, human-service agency that serves low-income people in the Waterloo, Ontario, area. He was ordained as a Mennonite pastor in 1977 and served at First Mennonite Church in Kitchener until 1996. In 2001 he began helping to form Interfaith Grand River, which promotes tolerance and religious diversity. He also worked in addiction counseling. He has published many articles and produced a number of videos on poverty, homelessness and other social issues. Brice was born in Dallas and grew up in Bluffton, Ohio. He holds graduate degrees from the University of St. Michael's College, Toronto, the University of Waterloo, and the Methodist Theological School in (Delaware) Ohio.